POST CAPITALIST
PHILANTHROPY

> ❝❞

"To my fellow colleagues in philanthropy: Many of us have begun to recognize that the current structures of our sector – and the beliefs they imprint upon us – don't truly serve the work we wish to shepherd. Well, buckle up! Herein lies the motherlode that can help us bring radical insight to the field. This is not a quick or easy read; it is a *tour de force* that asks us to do the hard work of cutting through conventional illusions that underpin the very worldview of philanthropy as we know it. The rich material offered here can lead us to a new way of seeing and to viable paths forward; what could be more important for our work and for our world?"

- Andrea Panaritis
Executive Director of *Christopher Reynolds Foundation*

"This book asks probing, deep questions about how philanthropy needs to heal itself if it has any chance of helping to heal our rift with the Earth, and in so doing profoundly challenges the complacent world of the financially wealthy to wake up, shake itself, and attempt to be truly meaningful to humanity's most important mission."

- Ashish Kothari
Co-editor of *Pluriverse: A post-development dictionary* and co-founder of *Global Tapestry of Alternatives*

"This book is the bone-rattling equivalent of a visit to the wild shaman's house: you'd suppose you made the brief trip to get some medicinal items, but there are often more things in their brew than are dreamt of in your plans. Tracing the ways that the modern philanthropic hand and the conditions of its possibility reinscribe neoliberal-traditionalist notions of agency, human centrality, and power, co-authors Ladha and Murphy conduct a sweeping and engaging ethnography of the archetypal, mythopoetic, institutional, and philosophical territories of capital as a worlding agent and as a carceral dynamic obscuring transformational possibilities. Their invitations to practice are rich; their message, potent – like a good shapeshifting brew: if we must address the unprecedented impasses of the modern civilizational project, we will need unprecedented modes of approach. We would need to move and think with our feet again, experimenting beyond money as a paradigm of control. *We've already begun.*"

- Bayo Akomolafe
Author, *These Wilds Beyond our Fences: Letters to My Daughter on Humanity's Search for Home* and founder of *The Emergence Network*

"This book blew me away: it's a soup to nuts primer on how to become a post-capitalist, in thought, action and spirit. One can only hope that today's philanthropists are ready for this necessary journey."

~ Carne Ross
Former UK diplomat; author of *The Leaderless Revolution*

"Alnoor and Lynn have thrown down a gauntlet: Time for philanthropy workers and owners of philanthropic resources to re-engage the relational and distribution contradictions in their life world, and to take deep stock of the mega-paradox at root in the support of democratic evolution through undemocratic ownership and management of wealth. They raise the critical question: Can philanthropy be leveraged to effect changes that make the world a safer and better place for all of us?"

~ Colin Greer
President of the *New World Foundation*

"Every day our world of capitalist modernity collapses a bit more, like mountains of Antarctic ice caving into the sea. But what to do about it? With a focus on philanthropy, this book dares to offer a vision commensurate with the scale of the problem. Ladha and Murphy astutely challenge the self-delusions of philanthrocapitalism and show how our many ecological crises have roots in our inner lives and culture. Read this book, expand your spiritual imagination, and nourish a richer sense of the possible!"

~ David Bollier
Director of the Reinventing the Commons Program at the *Schumacher Center for a New Economics*; author of *The Commoner's Catalog for Changemaking*

"This is an invitation to remember ourselves, as we forge a path towards a different way of being in life, with philanthropy as a lens to examine our predicament. Each page contained in this text is a reminder of what my heart already knows is true, with information and inspiration that lifts the sense of possibility for making deep change together."

~ Gail Bradbrook
Co-founder of *Extinction Rebellion*

"Philanthropy assumes that accumulated wealth can solve the big social and ecological crises of our time, when in reality these crises are an effect of accumulation itself. This book asks a daring question: can wealth be reappropriated to restore balance to our broken world? A key resource for anyone eager to rethink philanthropy and economics in the 21st century."

- **Jason Hickel**

Professor at the *Institute for Environmental Science and Technology, Barcelona (ICTA-UAB)*; Visiting Senior Fellow at the *London School of Economics*; author of *The Divide* and *Less is More*

"This is a book about the future of philanthropy that is unlike any other, encompassing spirituality and asking questions about what humanity itself is becoming. It is an illuminating journey into how we can each do better to rebuild the world."

- **Kumi Naidoo**

Former Secretary General of *Amnesty International*

"The potential of *Post Capitalist Philanthropy* is knowing when this "event" will happen, is happening, or has happened underneath our camouflaged terminology of politics, religion, and science. All Occidentally forced narratives are confined to searching for exit strategies of exoneration. This book is a direct challenge to prognosticators of worst-case scenarios. Will there be life after 'philanthropy' when the thinking patterns of dominance remain rooted in narcissistic systems of modernity? I can tell you the answers won't be found in the capitalism that invented the adamancy of control. Read on."

- **Tiokasin Ghosthorse**

Founder and host of *First Voices Radio*

"*Post Capitalist Philanthropy* is an essential mystical revolutionary handbook that should be required reading for anyone involved in philanthropy."

- **V (formerly Eve Ensler)**

Author of *The Vagina Monologues* and *The Apology*

POST CAPITALIST
PHILANTHROPY

-

THE HEALING OF WEALTH IN THE TIME OF COLLAPSE

Authors
ALNOOR LADHA & LYNN MURPHY

-

Foreword
DR VANDANA SHIVA

Artists
VITTORIA CARDONA
ALIXA GARCÍA & FEDERICO CRUZ

© 2023. This work is licensed under a Creative Commons Attribution-NonCommercial-ShareAlike 4.0 International License (CC 4.0 BY-NC-SA).

Published by Transition Resource Press / New York
Distributed by Daraja Press / Ottawa & Nairobi

Creative Direction & Design: Vittoria Cardona
Art work: Alixa García & Federico Cruz
Graphics: OCTOPI, South Africa
Research & Editing: Adam Oosthuizen

Library of Congress Cataloging-in-Publication Data

Ladha, Alnoor & Murphy, Lynn
Post Capitalist Philanthropy;
Healing Wealth in the Time of Collapse

ISBN 979-8-986531-00-7

Second edition, September 2023

...

May this text serve the healing of all beings, including the fallen deity of money, and its offspring, shadow and alibi, philanthropy. May the colonised mind and body be liberated, including our own.

TABLE OF CONTENTS

FOREWORD

GIFT ECONOMY & PHILANTHROCAPITALISM BY DR. VANDANA SHIVA XVII

PART ZERO | PARADOX BEFORE POSSIBILITY

PROLOGUE 2
CONTEXT 14
OBJECTIVES 18
GUIDING PRINCIPLES OF AN ON-GOING METHODOLOGY 22
WORKING PARADOXES 25
STRUCTURE OF THE TEXT 29

PART ONE | INTO THE PARADOX

THE FIRST HIERARCHY:
GLOBAL NEOLIBERAL OPERATING SYSTEM 36

THE SECOND HIERARCHY:
PHILANTHROPY AS EXTERNALITY OF NEOLIBERALISM 56

THE THIRD HIERARCHY:
INSTITUTIONS AS FRACTAL NODES UPHOLDING THE LOGIC OF PHILANTHROPY 70

THE FOURTH HIERARCHY:
INDIVIDUALS AS REPLICATORS OF NEOLIBERAL LOGIC 82

PART TWO | FROM PARADOX TO EMERGING POSSIBILITIES

CALLS FOR JUST TRANSITION 99
BEYOND JUST TRANSITION: JUSTICE PLUS ONTO-SHIFTS 112

PART THREE | FROM PYRAMID LOGIC TO SPIRAL LOGIC

COSMOLOGY AS THE CENTRE OF SPIRAL LOGIC	130
INDIVIDUAL BEINGS AS WEBS OF RELATIONAL ENTANGLEMENTS	138
INSTITUTIONS AS MEMBERS OF SOCIAL ECOLOGIES	146
PHILANTHROPIC SECTOR AS BIOME UNITING SOCIAL ECOLOGIES	151
FIVE ELEMENTS MANDALA	154
SUPERSTRUCTURE AS MYCELIAL SERVICE FOR VARIOUS BIOMES	168
EMBEDMENT WITHIN THE GAIAN ENTELECHY	184

PART FOUR | WALKING INTO THE UNKNOWN

SURRENDER, TRAVERSE, (RE)ENTER	200
MYTHO-POETIC EPILOGUE	208
CLOSING PRAYER / ACKNOWLEDGEMENTS	212

APPENDICES

GLOSSARY	214
BIBLIOGRAPHY	222
AUTHOR BIOGRAPHIES	241

FOREWORD

·

GIFT ECONOMY & PHILANTHROCAPITALISM

by DR. VANDANA SHIVA

Life is a gift.

The Earth gives us breath, water, nourishment: the gifts that are the currencies of life.

Our parents gave us the gift of our biological being. During the pandemic, everyone woke up again to the gift of care; the gift that had been made invisible and eclipsed by 500 years of colonialism and 300 years of colonial commerce frozen into mechanical, extractive systems of knowledge (a la Francis Bacon) and greed, selfishness and competition-based systems of economic life (enshrined in the logic of Adam Smith).

In this time of collapse, Alnoor Ladha and Lynn Murphy have brought us the gift of imagining other ways of thinking and living beyond the mechanistic paradigm of a dead, inert earth and the separation of humans from nature. Elsewhere I have called this way of being 'eco-apartheid'.

The mechanistic paradigm was central to the colonising mission. Today we know it to be out of tune with the ecological world based on interconnectedness, non-separation, vitality, and abundance spread through the gift economy. The quantum revolution of a century ago revealed the fractures of mechanistic thought. I once did my PhD on Hidden Variables and Non-locality in Quantum Theory. In contrast to the arrogance of certainty and mastery, the quantum world opens our horizons to uncertainty, non-separability and entanglement as the basis of our being. Ladha and Murphy refer to this notion as constituting one deep interconnection between ontology, epistemology and ethics. In this, they invoke Bohm's implicate order.

For me, knowing and doing have existed as one continuum. Noticing the interconnectedness of problems and possibilities amounts to true epistemic honesty and responsibility.

From the days of GATT and the WTO, I have been part of the movement challenging the perils of globalisation and participating in the *International Forum on Globalisation* (including the 1999 protests in Seattle which halted the WTO Ministerial).

In *Post Capitalist Philanthropy*, Ladha and Murphy walk us through the deep logics of neoliberalism, the foundations of globalisation and the ideology of corporate free trade. They remind us of how Margaret Thatcher wanted us to believe that "there is no society, only individuals" – in deep contrast to our lived realities of interbeing which tell us every moment that "there is no such thing as an individual."

Globalisation created billionaires, and billionaires are now directly trying to run the world through philanthropy.

I first woke up to the rise and rule of philanthrocapitalism in 2015 when I watched Bill Gates instruct heads of state about geo-engineering and genetic engineering as solutions to climate change at the *Paris Climate Summit*. It became clear to me at that moment that billionaires were not just economically powerful. They were now, politically speaking, more powerful than elected representatives. To better understand the emerging order of philanthrocapitalism and philanthropic imperialism I wrote 'Oneness vs 1%'.[1]

In 2020, the era of Covid began. The expansion of philanthrocapitalism into philanthro-imperialism was put on fast-forward. There was no aspect of everyday life that was not being rearranged and reset by the billionaires – from geo-engineering to manipulating the climate to engineering fake food in labs, from GMO soya to newly centralised systems of distribution for food and healthcare. In response, I invited movements I have worked with to contribute to a citizens' report entitled *Gates to a Global Empire* which was published as *Philanthrocapitalism and the Erosion of Democracy*.[2]

In brief, I see philanthrocapitalism as the new colonialism, the new enclosure of the commons.

In *Post Capitalist Philanthropy* the authors dissect philanthrocapitalism. And they indicate the possibilities of reclaiming the true economies of the gift, of solidarity, of caring and sharing. For now, I invite you to please read on as if Life depends on it.

Dr. Vandana Shiva
Dehradun, India

---

[1] Shiva, V. & Shiva, K. (2020)
[2] Shiva, V. (Ed.) (2022)

PART ZERO

PARADOX BEFORE POSSIBILITY

PARADOX BEFORE POSSIBILITY

PROLOGUE

~

*"How wonderful that we have met with a paradox.
Now we have some hope of making progress."*
- Niels Bohr

*"In the dark theopoetics of the cloud, might the very fold between our non-knowing
and our non-separability begin to appear [as] possibility itself, posse ipsum?"*
- Catherine Keller[3]

Post capitalist philanthropy is a paradox in terms. A paradox is the appropriate starting place for the complex, entangled, messy context we find ourselves in as a species. Those of us who are embedded in the muddled sub-sect of humans working in the sector known as philanthropy find ourselves pushed even further into contemplating the stark bifurcations of paradox.

There is a sheer irony in the act of arbitrarily giving away relatively small portions of money (compared to wealth holdings) derived from an unjust, extractive system within a philanthropic framework that enables tax-free, privately-controlled accumulations of assets, all in order to solve the very problems that wealth accumulation creates in the first place.[4] That such philanthropic actions take place within an economic operating system that is openly destroying our collective home

---
[3] Keller (2014), p.11. *Posse ipsum* is Latin for "possibility itself". Nicholas of Cusa, the 14th century German philosopher and mystic, refers to posse ipsum as "God as possibility itself."
[4] We will dive deeper into a historical/structural approach to analysing and understanding power and wealth further into the book. In the meantime, we ask you to sit with this question: what is just or deserved wealth within the current context?

– the Gaian ecosystem that maintains all of Life – can often feel like too much for any one soul to bear, especially without a framework or container for shared inquiry.

As such, we are embarking on a collective journey with no presumption of conclusions or certainties. At times, the content we offer may be provocative and challenging to some sensibilities and beliefs. This is why we will continually come back to the body and felt experience. We urge readers to take the time to sit with our exercises and contemplations rather than aiming to get to the last page or to find some kind of resolution.

This book is an opening salvo for a deeper dialogue – an admission of befuddlement and a cry for earnest inquiry. It is also a call for grief, outrage and humility amongst practitioners; an invitation to create emerging, embodied cultures; the opening of spaces for spiritual and political practice as on-going praxis; the reimagining of community-building amongst those working within and affected by this growing and powerful sector of philanthropy; and a provocation to become *contextually relevant* beings in troubled times.

Although the etymology of the term philanthropy simply means "the love of humanity", it has come to refer to an industry of non-governmental organisations that formally provide grants, ostensibly for public benefit. Much of the focus of this book is on institutional philanthropy, with a bias towards the United States, and to a lesser extent Europe, as these are still the centres of global neoliberalism in terms of both capital and cultural influence. Nevertheless, many of the observations and insights in this book can be applied to other geographies, other forms of social change work and to personal philanthropy (i.e. charitable giving) more broadly.

Institutional philanthropy cuts a wide swath. It encompasses the full political spectrum from conservative to progressive ideas on one continuum, and from "passive" (i.e. funding research work) to "active" (i.e. funding direct action) on the other. Regardless of political motivations or where funds are directed, the sector of philanthropy is an *externalisation of capitalism* – it is both a consequence and protection mechanism for the existing system. A small group of people have amassed large sums of wealth through an extractive system and then created a sector by which they can decide the agenda for civil society while receiving a multitude of publicly-conferred benefits (from tax breaks to lobbying power to social influence) that further concentrate private financial and social power.

Although this book is an inquiry into the possibilities of post capitalist realities more broadly, we mainly situate it within the context of philanthropy because this sector has the potential to play a critical role in rebalancing wealth, knowledge and power while repairing historical injustices. Yet, all too often, philanthropy exacerbates our current exploitative system through undemocratic and unaccountable processes; by increasing endowments through existing market mechanisms; and through a lack of imagination on how to support the requisite paradigm shifts.

As co-authors of this book, we have spent a cumulative forty-plus years giving grants, advising philanthropic organisations, and/or fundraising for political work. Over the past few years, we have set up a "temporary organisational zone" called the Transition Resource Circle to bring funders and activists into deeper dialogue about the liberatory potential of philanthropy.[5]

The word "transition" indicates the desired shift from the meta-crisis to transformative possibilities. "Resource" refers to the goal of alchemising and liberating capital in service to Life. And "circle" connotes ways of working which move us from hierarchical models and individual entitlements to honouring our collective entanglements. Through the *Transition Resource Circle*, we facilitate conversations through circle ways (e.g. non-hierarchical, embodied cognition approaches) so as to integrate the multiple intersections of our historical precedents, our respective lineages & storylines, and what future beings to come (including ourselves) require for reconciliation and healing.

This book is a direct result of these working lines, the fabric of relationships we steward, and our ongoing inquiries. What we have written in these pages is informed by our engagement with funders, activists, social movements, elders, cosmologists, anthropologists, economists, financial investors, business leaders, policy wonks and others. In addition, we conducted ongoing research of critical discourse in the space, hosted and led funder gatherings, and interviewed over a hundred people to inform this text.

---

[5] Borrowing from the notion of the temporary autonomous zone. See Bey (2003).

As we listened deeply to discussions of how philanthropy could lead a response to our current civilisational crisis, we found that no one person or group has "the answer". Instead, the conclusion we came to is that we must open up our inquiry to a broader audience than those working in philanthropy; we must ask those embedded in and affected by the sector to engage in fierce, honest conversations; to look deeper into how we see and make sense of the world; and to humble ourselves out of the certainty of answers. As such, this book is an offering and an invitation into collective sense-making at this critical crossroads.

Some of the questions we will sit with together as you engage with this text include: How can philanthropy help transform capitalism when it was created by the very contradictions and inequities stemming from the system? Would any desirable post capitalist future still include a sector called philanthropy? Would an elite few still have the power to decide the agenda of the civic life of others? And, importantly, why would anyone invested in the current system be interested in creating post capitalist realities, especially if this would mean having a smaller piece of the proverbial pie?

Before we start to deepen into these lines of inquiry, let's first discuss the use of the term *post capitalism*, which, within our context, is purposefully unspecific.

> *This book is an opening salvo for a deeper dialogue – an admission of befuddlement and a cry for earnest inquiry. It is also a call for grief, outrage and humility amongst practitioners; an invitation to create emerging, embodied cultures; the opening of spaces for spiritual and political practice as on-going praxis; the reimagining of community-building amongst those working within and affected by this growing and powerful sector of philanthropy; and a provocation to become contextually relevant beings in troubled times.*

WHAT IS POST CAPITALISM?

Post capitalism is an umbrella concept for us to better understand what we want to transition out of and transition into. Capitalism is not simply a system of market exchange. It is a system that measures and reduces the value of Life – including human labour, living ecosystems, relationships and life-force – via a crude system of transactional monetary exchange.

It is based on generating and accumulating ever-more commodified surplus value – i.e. more capital – by extracting, separating and abstracting currency from the human and more-than-human world. Capital is primarily created through debt, and therefore requires perpetual growth. Capitalism is a self-terminating algorithm based on socialising costs to the many while privatising gains for the few.

Post capitalism is not simply another 'ism' to replace previous ideologies. It is not a euphemism for socialism or anarchism or Nordic capitalism, although it may contain some elements of each. Post capitalism is a conceptual container for social pluralities based on *shared values* that stem from an experience of the shortcomings of the existing system and the lived experience of life-centric alternatives.

Some of the core uniting values of this idea include: reciprocity, altruism, cooperation, gratitude, gifting, regeneration, equity consciousness, communalism, shared governance & decision-making, empathy, non-violence, interbeing and solidarity with all Life. In short, we are endeavouring to find approaches, practices and models that usher in systems rooted in interconnected relationships and a broader honouring of Life, in all its diversity and mystery.

We do not include a dash between 'post' and 'capitalism' in order to make clear that it is not simply a temporal state that exists *after* capitalism. Post capitalist realities exist right now, and many have existed for hundreds (if not thousands) of years despite the dominant system(s). For example, Indigenous cultures and communities that are based in the values mentioned above are inherently post capitalist even if they were not created in opposition to capitalism; their very existence is a form of resistance in the face of the dominant culture's desire to eradicate and undermine them.

Resistance movements such as the Zapatistas in Mexico and Rojava in Kurdistan are already living post capitalist realities. As authors, we have an explicit desire to help create contexts that cultivate more experiments and support existing, emerging possibilities. This is what we mean by *post capitalist futures*. We acknowledge they are here now, and some have always been here. There will be more (their challenge to the dominant system is inevitable), and these realities do not require any future end-state to be validated.[6]

This also does not mean these experiments are operating "outside" of capitalism or in a "pure" state, because, as we will discuss, there is not necessarily an "outside" – either materially or metaphysically. Late-stage capitalism is the water we swim in and we are all entangled in the consequences to our ecosystem, nervous systems, food systems, communities, relationships, waterways, psychological conditioning and our very life-force.

Although the prefix *post* can imply a "context after", it also implies a state which is informed by the context prior to it. This is why understanding the dominant system is so critical. If we do not have a clear perspective of capitalism, we become contextually irrelevant. However, if all we have is a critique of the dominant system, we in turn become spiritually and creatively impoverished. This is why post capitalism is a necessary discourse for the collective imaginary.

Within our working definition, post capitalist realities are possible pathways that share the following principles:

- POST ANTHROPOCENTRIC
  Beyond the human-centric gaze and species exceptionalism, and towards the valuing of all Life.

- TRANS-RATIONALIST
  Where rationality is incorporated but not elevated beyond other ways of knowing, sensing and being.

---

[6] Our deep gratitude to Gustavo Esteva for reminding us of the fallacy of linear time in the creation/existence of post capitalist realities. Gustavo passed away during the publication of this book on March 17, 2022. He was an elder, ally, mentor, comrade and a member of the Accompaniment Circle for the Transition Resource Circle. May peace be upon him.

- POST TRANSACTIONAL
  Where acts of exchange are based on relational acts of genuine connection, reciprocity, generosity, cooperation and solidarity.

- ANTI-PATRIARCHAL
  Where gender or sexual orientation do not determine socio-economic or cultural hierarchies.

- POST HIERARCHICAL
  There may be functional, fluid hierarchies agreed upon by members of relevant constituencies without domination, coercion or violence.

- ANTI-COLONIALIST
  Where systems and cultures are created to prevent widespread domination, extraction and/or imposition of worldviews onto "others".

- ANTI-RACIST
  Acknowledging the structural disparities and inequities brought about by the construct of race, white supremacist culture and its historical antecedents, while structuring new-ancient-emerging systems[7] that honour differences and seek to integrate reparations and reconciliation.

As the reader/practitioner/editor/co-creator of this text, you will have to decide which of the many constraints and limits to our dominant forms of capitalism most concern and animate you, what post capitalism could mean to you, how you will contribute to its creation, what values you will centre in your articulation of new-ancient-emerging states, and how, if at all, philanthropy will play a role in the coming transition(s) and creation of post capitalist realities.

---

[7] We will use the term new-ancient-emerging throughout this text to signify the synthesis of the temporal trinity of past, present and future as a non-linear phenomenon where there are no tidy delineations between the three phases. We use new as the prefix in order to uproot the dominant cultural notion that 'new' is most desirable; rather, we suggest that what is 'new' is also the most immature, requiring both an ancient, historical lens and an emergent becoming that we do not yet know.

We are not approaching our analysis, suggestions or questions with a sense of certainty, even though it may feel like this at times (especially when we render a picture of the current context). If you disagree with our approach or content as you read this text, we encourage you to notice more precisely what you disagree with and 'why' rather than just the 'what', and note moreover where the disagreement lands in your body.

You can also pause along the way for moments of reflection and somatic tracking. Of course, feel free to skip pages or sections that do not resonate, although we invite you to stay with any discomforts that may arise as we often learn most deeply in places of dissonance. Our endeavour is not to convince you of our arguments; rather, we are gesturing towards ways in which each of us can deepen into inquiry and embody practices of other ways of knowing, sensing and being.

MYTHO-POETIC PROLOGUE

Before we delve into our subjective reconnaissance of the current crisis, it feels proper to start with a foray into the realm of the mytho-poetic. Mythology has the unique ability to access deeper truths beyond rational argumentation, to speak the languages of imagination and possibility, and to access parts of our psyches through archetypal knowledge & shared memory.[8]

Our journey begins in Ancient Egypt, with the culture's most important deity: Osiris, the god of *Duat*, the Underworld. Some readers will be familiar with aspects of the Osiris mythos. He is the god of judgement who decides which souls will enjoy eternal life in the *Duat* (which is more akin to the Judeo-Islamic-Christian conception of heaven). The jackal god Anubis brings the souls of the deceased to Ma'at, the god of divine justice. She then weighs each soul against a feather. If the soul is lighter than the feather, Horus, the son of Osiris, brings that soul to his father for final judgement.

---

[8] We refer to archetypes as conceptualised and defined by Carl Jung. Archetypes are primal symbols and images derived from the "collective unconscious", the shared repository of cumulative knowledge. Archetypal knowledge is derived from human history, which foreshadows and can direct conscious behaviour.

Many will also be familiar with the betrayal aspect of the Osiris mythology. Osiris' brother Set, the god of violence and chaos, was jealous of his brother's role presiding over the Underworld. According to one rendition of the myth, Set built an ornate, bejewelled coffin and announced to the court of gods: "Whoever fits into the coffin will keep it as their own." The various gods then attempted and failed to fit in the confines of the coffin, until, of course, Osiris lay inside it. Set immediately locked the coffin, cut it into 14 pieces and threw the constitutive pieces into the Nile, thereby securing Osiris's throne. Thus, Set became the pharaoh of pharaohs.

Osiris' wife and sister Isis, along with their sister Nepthys, searched for years for the various pieces, often invoking the support of the other gods. Finally, Isis reconstructed Osiris, finding his remaining limbs embedded in a tamarisk tree trunk holding up the roof of a palace in Byblos. But she could not find his phallus. With the use of magic, she created a golden phallus, attached it to his body, and resurrected him by making love to him. This union of the feminine (the ongoing search, the reconstruction) with the masculine will brought about Osiris' resurrection and the continuation of life through the creation of Horus, the falcon-winged god that eventually took his father's place as Lord of the Worlds and avenged his father's death by killing his uncle Set.[9]

The aspect of the mythos that is not commonly known is how Osiris became a god in the first place.[10] This part starts with humble beginnings. Osiris was once a shepherd and a farmer going about his work in the fields. In some interpretations, he was struck by lightning, through which he accessed a hypnagogic state that sent him down to the Underworld where he traversed the seven houses of challenge or gates of initiation. In Normandi Ellis' poetic interpretation of the *Book of the Dead*, Osiris responds with animistic eloquence as he is confronted by the various guardians of each gate – the gods and monsters who question his right to ascension.[11]

---

[9] Budge & Wilson (Eds.) (2016)

[10] Through the Pyramid Texts, the first Egyptian funerary texts, which appeared on the walls of burial chambers in pyramids at the end of the Fifth Dynasty, around 2400 BCE, the Coffin Texts from the Middle Kingdom (circa 2055 to 1650 BCE) and the Book of the Dead from the New Kingdom (circa 1550 to 1070 BCE), the origin myth of Osiris has been reconstructed to tell the further story.
See Budge & Wilson (Eds.) (2016).

[11] Ellis (1988)

Osiris enters the first gate by declaring his divinity and humility: "Let me pass! ... I am a spirit walking in darkness by the light of his own divinity ... I am a worshipper of light ... Show me the ways of change...."[12]

The second gate is the "walls of misconception", including ignorance, anger, and forgetfulness, which Osiris must face with truth, strength and love. He declares: "I shall ease the pain and sorrow of gods with the sweet pods of carob trees, with the fragrant perfume of memory, with the pungent odour of love."[13]

At the third gate, he confronts two jackals and a serpent god entwined with a stalk of corn. Here he must affirm his fearlessness and his fidelity to the divine throughout his life. He states: "I have cast out sadness. I have thrown down fear... I have done what the gods willed for me... In all my thoughts, I chiselled the gods' names and the words of power were set into stone."[14]

The fourth gate demands his annunciation of fidelity to his own being, to Truth itself. Osiris decrees: "I am the heart of Osiris... I am a scribe faithful to the language of the heart...I have judged the guilt in my own heart, cut out its defects and burned them in fire."[15]

The fifth challenge demands that Osiris must prove his loyalty to his ancestors and show himself capable of integrating the various aspects of himself into wholeness. He states: "I have gathered my opposites, my fragmented thoughts, desires and flesh... I am the thousand sparks of fire returning, becoming one with flame... Grant me passion along the way that I may complete my becoming."[16]

He then approaches the sixth house of challenge, the gateway of sacrifice of the self for greater wisdom. He faces three drunken dogs who snap at anyone trying to scale the walls. Osiris announces: "I carry the crown of existence, the man I became... through will and devotion and action, through determination to walk in truth with light. I have seen the great world and the small one. I gave my sight to the gods and the gods gave me visions... Let me pass for my journey is nearly complete. It is not the end of the path, but its source, the beginning. I walk on in the heart of god."[17]

---

[12] Ellis (1988), p.62
[13] Ibid, p.63
[14] Ibid, p.64
[15] Ibid, p.65
[16] Ibid, p.65
[17] Ibid, p.66

Finally, he approaches the seventh gate, the gate of judgement, where he must face himself. He sees a lion and a hare whose crossed swords meet, blocking his way. Between the two he sees an old man, a guardian smiling back at him as his mirror twin. Osiris says to himself: "I have come home bringing my soul... I speak of things of matter, the life that possessed this body, and though I pass away, these things do not but live in me. I carry into heaven the life of Earth... I am I – an old man become strong, a tongue spitting light into darkness."[18]

As he passes, he is challenged by a snake.

> "The snake observed me with amber eyes. He motioned toward a door that opened from air into air."
>
> "Can your heart name the name of this gate?"
>
> "Being," I said.
>
> "And the lands on either side?"
>
> "Creation and destruction."
>
> "Pass then, Osiris," he said.[19]

Here Osiris accepts the world in its full shadow in order to truly honour the gift of existence. He must see with his heart beyond his own being, he must perceive both sides – creation and destruction. His is a path of grave difficulty and uncertainty. Even after he passes the final gate, he does not enter eternal heavenly bliss. Rather, he is unsure of where he is and what will happen next. He ponders aloud: "Is it even the same road I travelled a moment ago? I walk on Earth again in the light — or is it heaven, another circular path? I change and change again. I am a god and the ways lie open, all the paths of my various becomings... The journey ahead stays uncertain. I am the essence of what I am, travelling the back of a snake."[20]

---

[18] Ellis (1988), pp.67-68
[19] Ibid, p.150
[20] Ellis (1988), p.67

It was not enough that Osiris declared his divinity and humility, transcended ignorance, faced his fears, proved his fidelity to the gods, honoured his ancestors, and offered sacrifice for illumination. He also had to face himself. He could not simply declare to the gods the beauty of his earthly experience or his light, he had to "speak of things of matter"; he had to understand the consequences of his actions and be willing to judge that which he did not condone, *to spit light into darkness.*

This is no new-age fairy tale of the simple acceptance of 'what is', or non-judgement. Countless other humans managed to pass one or more of these gates, but Osiris was the only mortal to pass all seven to become a god. He became the god of judgement because he was not only willing to say what he stood for, but also what he stood against.

Osiris exercises a divine discontent through his judgement, understanding that consequence is both the grammar and currency of the gods. Osiris understands judgement in non-dualistic terms. He understands that fear of judgement or duality can create and perpetuate duality. Later in the *Book of the Dead*, he states: "When you've reached the lips of the great devourer, you are staring into the jaws of creation."[21]

Creation and destruction are two ends of the same equation. Osiris and Set are aspects of each other. This worldview holds an appreciation of the necessity of the various actors and archetypes required for the cosmic drama to unfold. This is judgement without charge, without personalisation. Judgement without supremacy. It is a refined spirit-math, a quantum ethic, a celestial calculus beyond rationalism, materialism and positivism.

With this prologue, let us venture into a different kind of underworld: the context of late-stage capitalism.

---

[21] Ibid, p.129

CONTEXT

~

We are in the midst of a *meta-crisis*: ecological collapse, climate change, species extinction, increasing pandemics, institutional racism, rising authoritarianism, spiking inequality and inhumane poverty. All of these consequences are the logical outcome of our dominant economic, political, and cultural system.

Since 1980, about 46% of all economic growth has gone to the richest 5% of humanity.[22] Only 5% of this new wealth over the same period has ended up in the hands of the world's majority – 60% of humanity.[23] Therefore, by definition, growth actively creates economic inequality. Economic growth requires that an ever-shrinking minority of people extract more from the natural world and from the bodies of an ever-expanding mass of people.

The economic anthropologist Jason Hickel takes this point further in relation to income: "The richest 1% alone capture $19 trillion in income every year, which represents nearly a quarter of global GDP. That adds up to more than the GDP of 169 countries *combined* – a list that includes Norway, Sweden, Switzerland, Argentina, all of the Middle East and the entire continent of Africa. The rich lay claim to an almost unimaginable share of the income the global economy generates; income that is extracted from the lands and bodies of the poor."[24]

Also, every dollar of wealth created heats up our planet, as the global system is built upon an extractives-based fossil fuel economy. More growth requires more energy, which requires more demand for fossil fuels and makes it even more difficult to decarbonise energy systems. To the extent that capitalism requires growth, it generates and exacerbates climate change and ecological breakdown.[25] It inevitably does so to the detriment of future generations of human and more-than-human beings.

---

[22] World Inequality Database (2017)
[23] See Woodward (2015), pp.43-52
[24] Hickel (2020), p.192
[25] Klein (2015), p.25

Capitalism invariably leads to what the ecological sociologist William Catton calls *overshoot*. He states: "Human beings, in two million years of cultural evolution, have several times succeeded in taking over additional portions of the Earth's total life-supporting capacity, at the expense of other creatures. Each time, the human population has increased. But man has now learned to rely on a technology that augments human-carrying capacity in a necessarily temporary way – as temporary as the extension of life by eating the seeds needed to grow next year's food."[26]

Within the context of the existing operating system, no amount of reform, whether it be green investment or otherwise, can change the structure and trajectory of the self-terminating, exponential function of growth-based capitalism.

Scientists and policy experts almost unanimously agree that we will not be able to meet the global targets for keeping global warming to less than 1.5 degree celsius by 2050 if we carry on with the status quo of our economic system.[27] Our current trajectory has us on track for a three degree rise in temperature before the end of the century. It is important though to note that these are conservative estimates, from organisations like the United Nations, the World Bank and other establishment entities, who are incentivised not to alarm the general population and disrupt the current equilibrium.

We cannot even fathom what a planet warmed by three degree celsius will look like. It will wipe out 30% to 50% of existing species; sea levels will rise by two to ten metres; more than 1.5 billion people will be displaced as climate refugees. We will experience massive global droughts, uninhabitable oceans, and runaway, cascading feedback loops. We read about the climate crisis, live through its catastrophes, and we often plainly see how capitalism is driving us towards extinction, and yet we are still somehow disconnected from its very real near-term implications. This human attribute has been described by psychologists as "temporal myopia" – a time-blindness rooted in our evolutionary problem-solving capabilities.[28]

Despite the stark material reality of these cascading collapses, economists, bankers and the financial orthodoxy continually reiterate that within the current debt/growth

---

[26] Catton (1982), p.19
[27] Buis (2019)
[28] van der Wal, van Horen and Grinstein (2018)

system, we must grow the global economy at 3% a year to avoid stagnation and/or recession. This is because growth has to exceed interest rates in order for the debt-based money (which is loaned into existence) to return both principal and interest. Three per cent may not sound like much, but it requires a doubling of the global economy every 23 years.[29] We have already crossed six of the nine planetary boundaries and are in the midst of the Sixth Great Extinction: a doubling of the global economy is now a material impossibility.[30]

As such, we have to create new contexts and structures that shift our entire civilisation's approach to consumption and production. If this wasn't enough, we have the amplifying urgency of time itself; we have perhaps ten to twenty years left of our consumption-based way of living on this current trajectory. The conservative scientific consensus is that we have ten years to cut global emissions in half to stay under 1.5 degrees of warming. At the current rate, widespread uninhabitability for human life will occur by 2070, although this is already occurring in many places in the global South and may happen even sooner in the global North.[31]

Of course, this is a linear timeline and human response and integration to each successive phase of the coming transition(s) will (co)determine how these changes play out; however, economists tell us there will not be another doubling of the global economy; ecologists warn us that we have crossed critical thresholds and continue to do so with no signs of slowing down; and energy and policy analysts remind us that this brief window of fossil fuel abundance, sometimes called the "carbon pulse", is already coming to an end.[32]

As we will argue, one of our key propositions is the notion that the meta-crisis is not something outside of us. All of us who are embedded in capitalist modernity are complicit (to varying degrees of course) in perpetuating the dominant culture.[33]

---

[29] Hickel (2020)
[30] Wang-Erlandsson, Tobian, van der Ent, Fetzer, te Wierik, Porkka, Staal, et al. (2022)
[31] Chi, Kohler, Lenton, Svenning & Scheffer (2020)
[32] This is a term borrowed from energy analyst and political philosopher Nate Hagens. For a deeper dive into the carbon pulse and where our use of it is taking us, see Hagens (2019).
[33] Capitalist modernity is a term borrowed from Abdullah Öcalan's now classic text, *Manifesto for a Democratic Civilization: The Age of Masked Gods and Disguised Kings*. We will use the term interchangeably with neoliberalism, late-stage capitalism and other descriptors of our current paradigm. The advantage of the term *capitalist modernity* is that it refers to both the political economy and the

Philanthropy believes it is part of the solution. And sometimes it is. However, we believe that the philanthropic sector requires a radical re-imagining of its purpose, capabilities and the possibilities for intervention in the wake of the current context.

We believe that the wealth currently concentrated and privately held in the hands of increasingly few (and within the unaccountable, occluded sector of philanthropy) is truthfully the world's shared, collective endowment, which includes many aspects of wealth beyond money. This shared wealth has been built on the backs of countless generations and an accretion of human, and more-than-human, destruction and sacrifice. We see ethical, moral and karmic implications in the choices each of us make, and especially the decisions of those in seats of power and privilege in times of exponential change and collapse. Rather than wealth holders having an inherent right to make decisions on how this communal wealth should be allocated, we see a burden with disproportionate responsibility that has consequences that cannot be understood from our current vantage point.

As such, one of the key inquiries of this book is how we might redefine collective responsibility. How do we create systems that invite others, especially those most affected by the decisions of philanthropy, to co-steward the future of wealth? What are some of the personal implications of being a money hoarder at the end of our current epoch? What does it mean to be a gate-keeper in a time of great suffering? What does it mean to be an ally to those that history has forsaken? What does it mean to support the efforts of those our ancestors harmed as redemption work? We do not hold the answers to these questions, nor do we posit that these are the only questions that matter. Rather, we are suggesting that contemplation is in order. There is more to this business of philanthropy than meets the eye.

> *Rather than wealth holders having an inherent right to make decisions on how this communal wealth should be allocated, we see a burden with disproportionate responsibility that has consequences that cannot be understood from our current vantage point.*

deeper cultural projects of colonialism, imperialism, positivism, rationalism and materialism, i.e. the project of a totalising modernity based on separation from the living world. See Öcalan (2015).

OBJECTIVES

~

Albert Camus famously described his classic text *The Myth of Sisyphus* as "a lucid invitation to live and to create in the very midst of the desert."[34] Our starting point here is the recognition that living within the dominant culture is, by definition, living within a metaphorical desert – spiritually, economically, politically, intellectually, directionally, cosmologically, linguistically, emotionally, sensorily, psychologically and in ways we cannot imagine. Although there are communities that live outside of the desert, outside the logic of late-stage capitalism, the dominant system is increasingly affecting all geographies, biomes, cultures and peoples. To continue with the tradition of Camus, this book is a lucid invitation to live, create, dream and, perhaps, die well, in the midst of the desert of capitalist modernity.

The increasing monoculture of our physical environment and of our cognitive/spiritual capacities is quickening at such a pace that all living beings are implicated in the consequences of what is happening and what is to come. We can call this moment in history the meta-crisis, the poly-crisis, civilisational collapse, the great transition, the great unravelling, the Anthropocene, the Kali Yuga[35], or any other descriptor (some of these we will use interchangeably); however, its weight and

---

[34] Camus (2018), p.3

[35] In the Vedic tradition of India, the Kali Yuga is the fourth and final yuga (world age) in the great Yuga Cycle. It is preceded by the Treta Yuga (Silver Age) then the Dvapara Yuga (Bronze Age) and followed by the Satya Yuga (Golden Age). It is widely considered that we are currently within the Kali Yuga. This is reflected in other cosmologies, including the Hopi prophecy of the Sixth Sun; the Iroquois Seventh Fire; the Age of Degeneration in Buddhism; and the Time of the Underworld in Alchemical thought. We recommend Sri Yukteswar Giri's (2013) book, *The Holy Science*. Sri Yukteswar uses a 24,000 year cycle with a 12,000 year ascending cycle and a 12,000 year descending cycle. The four ages are respectively 4800, 3600, 2400 and 1200 years long. As such, the Kali Yuga is the shortest cycle. According to many Vedic astrologers, we are nearing the end of the Kali Yuga, which also means that humans will receive the most support from the more-than-human realms. We are not suggesting this to be "true" or "fact" but simply another way of knowing and being that may help with contextualising our current moment. It is also important to acknowledge that Hindu nationalism has co-opted many aspects of Vedic thought, including the notion of the Kali Yuga, to perpetuate unspeakable crimes against marginalised communities in India, including Dalits, Muslims, and others.

directionality are clear. We are entering into an abyss of unknown consequences and unfathomable magnitude, driven by systems built upon human exceptionalism, callous extraction, selfish consumption, fearful racism, perpetual violence, soaring inequalities, authoritarian hierarchies, domination of all kinds and sheer absurdity.

This book is not an attempt to engage in the fool's errand of solving the multiple paradoxes or providing answers; this is not a policy paper or set of recommendations with a clear-eyed view of the future as a monolithic event horizon that can be seen and understood in its entirety from our present vantage point. This is not a celebration of frameworks, tools or theories (though a few will be presented in the hopes of offering inspiration to be remixed and/or discarded). This is not a rationalist attempt at meaning-making.

Rather, we are attempting to situate philanthropy within the broader global context so as to better understand why philanthropy is not responding in a commensurate, or arguably, meaningful way in the face of so many clear data points telling us that we are on the verge, and in the midst, of a civilisational collapse. Despite the growing global justice movement(s) centred on equity and redistribution, there is a growing and egregious amount of wealth being amassed by a small group of people and in the endowments of foundations.

Philanthropy, and the social change sector at large, are clinging to outdated ontological views about how change happens. At best, they are reinforcing the status quo, and often, deepening the meta-crisis.[36] Despite the growing discourse about systems change, by and large, philanthropy continues to reify its traditional levers of change – policy, innovation, advocacy, measurement, outcome-oriented strategies, positivist research, and other 'safe' avenues.

This book is partly an inquiry into how we breach the dearth of ideas in philanthropy and address the deeper logics of the dominant system, and its subsection of philanthropy. We are also exploring the means by which we might speak truth in ways that can be heard by those affected by philanthropy (e.g. civil society, social movements, etc.)

---

[36] We introduce the notion of ontology further on. The concept refers to the ways in which we understand the world, its "beingness" and its "becomingness", including our role as humans within the unfolding reality.

while attempting to bridge the divide between *wealth holders* and *wealth granters* in order to begin to let go of power, wealth, status, and other traditional desires so we can better collectively navigate an increasingly uncertain future.[37]

Reading, writing and interpreting this text is in itself an attempt to practise *non-dualistic thinking* and *embodied cognition*. Non-dualism here refers to the ability to hold two or more simultaneous and seemingly conflicting points-of-view. It is our ability to acknowledge the vast desert that has been created in this epoch of the Anthropocene, while acknowledging that we are not all feeling the implications in the same way; that we can be both inside and outside destruction at the same time; that we are all complicit in both the darkness and the light, no matter where we are situated. We can be both poison and medicine. We can be both the patient and the healer. And we often play many archetypal roles simultaneously.

Embodied cognition is the practice of moving from purely rational thought (which, from a trauma perspective, is often a dissociative state) into the felt, somatic experience of lived bodily realities. It is also non-dualistic in the sense that we are not exacerbating Cartesian mind-body splits, but, rather, invoking a discursive process where thought can shape one's body and its positionality in the world, and vice versa. Rather than setting thinking as the only starting place for understanding experience, the body also informs the mind – re-calibrating experience through mind-body sense-making in a dialogic, non-linear manner.

The old binaries – mind versus body, spirit versus matter, secular versus sacred, public versus private, rational versus irrational, left versus right, culture versus nature, transcendent versus immanent – are falling apart; perhaps they always were. Rather than placing rationality at the pinnacle of human thought, we are invoking a *trans-rational, multi-sensorial approach* that incorporates instincts, somatic responses, felt experiences, epigenetics, ancestral whispers and other phenomena that we do not fully know how to describe.

You will see that we attempt to centre other ways of knowing, sensing and being; other languages, cosmologies, ontologies, and approaches outside of the Western, linear, axiomatic, worldview.

---

[37] We distinguish between wealth holders and wealth granters later on in the text.

Although we do not have answers, we are gesturing towards a more *animistic worldview* in which the universe, the planet, and the fractals of their composite parts, including ourselves, and the bacteria we are made of, are engaged in dialectic dialogue, self-reflective awareness, and consciousness-producing processes. In some ways, this is the opposite of the neoliberal logic laid out by the former UK Prime Minister Margaret Thatcher when she infamously said: "There is no such thing as society".[38] In critical ways, from our internal bacteria to the social construction of reality, *there is no such thing as the individual.* Thus, we are invoking a relational web of being and becoming.

Rather than seeing the world as dead matter, or the human as a rational agent, or philanthropy as a set of logical and financial decisions to maximise the effectiveness of money, we are acknowledging the primacy of entanglement, of multiple simultaneous ontologies outside the human realms of understanding. We are attempting to transcend the separation of ethics, epistemology and ontology in a more deeply embedded *ethico-onto-epistemology*, to borrow Karen Barad's long but necessary phrasing.[39] In essence, we are aiming to create a coherence between how we understand the world, how we see the world, and how we act accordingly.

> *Although we do not have answers, we are gesturing towards a more animistic worldview in which the universe, the planet, and the fractals of their composite parts, including ourselves, and the bacteria we are made of, are engaged in dialectic dialogue, self-reflective awareness, and consciousness-producing processes.*

---

[38] Thatcher (September, 23 1987)

[39] Karen Barad's term, Ethico-onto-epistemology, suggests that what is in the world (ontology) and how we know what is in the world (epistemology), and how we navigate our morality amongst being and knowing are not separate, but emerge materially in an ongoing dynamic. That is, the nature of reality, the nature of knowledge, and the nature of ethics are entangled, not fixed or final or determinate. In a fuller sense, none of these can be divorced from power and what we find valuable or just, so to write about an 'onto-ethico-politico-epistemology' is probably more appropriate, but no less infuriating, so we'll keep the Baradian triad alive for the duration of this text. See Barad (2007).

For simplicity's sake, we will occasionally replace *ethico-onto-epistemology* with the language of *onto-shift*, drawing on the work of David Bollier and Silke Helfrich in their important book, *Free, Fair and Alive: The insurgent power of the commons*.[40] Although Bollier and Helfrich did not initially frame their definition of *onto-shift* in this way, we have asked their permission to remix their language in the spirit of creative commons.

We are attempting to practise and model post capitalist values through the language, processes and understandings we employ in this inquiry. Although there is no correct way to deepen this practice, we are attempting to enact an *on-going spiritual-political praxis* with the aim of becoming more *contextually sensitive* in order to become more *contextually relevant* to the current moment of interconnected collapses, the meta-crisis, the Anthropocene, the Kali Yuga. We are deepening our practice of being in dialogue with the animate world, "to meet the universe halfway" (to borrow Barad's language)[41], and, critically, to create the silent space of listening that allows this dialogue to emerge.

GUIDING PRINCIPLES FOR AN ON-GOING METHODOLOGY

~

One of the critical starting places for understanding a methodology generally is to understand who is writing this book, and for what purpose. Although we do not want to reify our personal identities, it is important to state that the co-authors are two subjective beings who carry with them personal biases, influenced and influenceable perspectives, historical traumas, epigenetic phenomena, ancestral forces and other influences that we do not fully understand.

---

[40] Bollier & Helfrich (2019). Silke tragically died in a hiking accident in November 2021 as we were writing the first draft of this book. She was a pioneer and a beacon for the commons movement and all others defending life-centric ways of being. May peace be upon her. We recommend reading David Bollier's remembrance of her, see Bollier (November 16, 2021).

[41] Barad (2007)

These subjectivities in turn affect and shape the output of the research. If you would like to know more about the co-authors, please see the biographies section at the end of the book. We have also worked with our Accompaniment Circle – an editorial, research and conceptualising advisory board of eleven allies/elders with all relevant experience who have helped guide and shape the writing process.[42]

There are currently eight guiding principles that form our ongoing methodology:

1. We acknowledge that our subjective sense-making activities involve somatic, cognitive, psychological, political and spiritual processes that are determined and limited by the character of those holding the inquiries. Sense-making is contextually determined, and our subjectivity is part of the context.

2. Part of our practice is to help both the "authors" and "readers" deepen their understanding of the larger context of global uncertainty and scenarios of collapse, with no expectation that we will achieve "final answers". We are gesturing towards *coordinates of possibility* rather than fixed conclusions. As Jurgen Habermas recently stated: "There never was so much knowing about our not-knowing and about the constraint to act and live in uncertainty."[43]

3. We are attempting to develop and strengthen *currently atrophied muscles* for engaging with non-dualistic thought and embodied cognition, as we attempt to hold multiple, simultaneous realities and seemingly conflicting ideas that live with and through our bodies. Our main objectives are not consistency, clarity or linearity. As Ralph Waldo Emerson famously stated: "A foolish consistency is the hobgoblin of little minds, adored by little statesmen and philosophers and divines."[44]

4. We centre our work on the relationality of beings, including the more-than-human realm. Wherever possible, we focus on relationships rather than efficiency or objective answers. To paraphrase David Abram, *there is no objective truth, there is only the quality of relationships.*[45]

---

[42] You can find biographies for our Accompaniment Circle at www.transitionresourcecircle.org.
[43] Lenel (2020)
[44] Emerson (September 4, 2005), p.90
[45] Abram (2012)

5. Envisioning and creating post capitalist futures is an emergent process that will not be determined by any one person, perspective, or process. Nor can the most pluralistic approach truly incorporate the needs/desires of all possible communities, peoples, geographies, unseen forces and other agencies. We try to presence our blindspots throughout the process, even if we cannot address them directly.

6. Language is inherently limited. Especially written language, and, even more so, the descendants of Proto-Indo-European languages. English, for example, is inherently binary and oppositional in its structure, and is mediated with particular biases, especially through its heavy reliance on nouns. This creates a world of subjects versus objects, creating an "objectification" of the animate world. Therefore, English can only describe the world in an extremely limited way. We acknowledge these limitations, although we cannot fully comprehend the extent or ways in which we are limited, nor the impacts of this upon our own consciousness. As Meister Eckhart reminds us, "all language has taken an oath to fail."[46]

7. We do not have an agenda in a traditional sense. We are publishing this content under a *Creative Commons* licence without charge for the online version. The proceeds from the hard copy will be used to support our not-for-profit and make our in-person gatherings accessible for activists, elders and others. Our aim is not to persuade the reader of our point-of-view; rather, this text is an invitation to collectively deepen our inquiries into the subject matter at hand.

8. In order to make our work richer and more collaborative, we will continuously broaden the circle of beings we are in dialogue with so we can better listen and root ourselves in humility, reciprocity, and rigour so that our process can be coherent with our inquiry (to the best of our ability, as we endeavour to embody decolonial practices and thought-forms). In this sense, we are engaging with *living theory* and are being shaped by it, for better or worse.

We start with these guiding principles to signpost our lines of inquiry, the manner by which we approach, the ways in which we listen, and how we synthesise, analyse, and generate ideas into what philanthropy can be and what we ourselves need to do

---

[46] Ladinsky (2002), p.97

and become in order to better serve post capitalist, life-centric ways of living. We do not approach this work with a sense of certainty or knowing, except that we know we will not achieve our expectations or fulfil pre-conditioned desires.

WORKING PARADOXES

~

Our starting place for our methodology and inquiry is paradox as the entry point to contemplate and enact non-dualistic thought and embodied cognition.

Below are some of the paradoxes we continue to grapple with. You will find the traces of the tensions of these paradoxes and apparent contradictions throughout this text.

1. *Paradox of personality* – We want to both acknowledge the role of individual personalities and their subjective influences, while deepening into non-identified states of being. Our individual personalities, preferences and identities are both paramount to sense-making and obstacles for the deepening of understanding, empathy, and the transcension of subject/object duality. Relatedly, even though this text points to a shared complicity in the dominant culture, there are some people who are more complicit than others and are actively benefiting from the meta-crisis. This acknowledgment is part of non-dualistic thought. Even at an archetypal level, there may be a 1%er in all of us, yet there is still agency, responsibility and consequence for every individual choice we make.

2. *Paradox of practice* – The more we practise emerging forms of sense-making, the better we become at holding complex, non-dualistic thoughts. Yet we become ignorant in other ways we cannot see. Albert Einstein was once quoted as saying: "As our circle of knowledge expands, so does the circumference of darkness surrounding it."

3. *Paradox of power* – As we value other ways of knowing and being, we situate power outside the traditional conceptions. Yet, the powers of wealth, decision-making, status, racialised hierarchies, and other systems of oppression continue to affect the

lives of all of us, and indeed, all of Life. For example, the more we as co-authors are embedded within the halls of philanthropy or situated in proximity to traditional power, the less effective we will become at valuing other modalities of power.

4. *Paradox of privilege* – Although there can be an acknowledgement of privilege (e.g. economic, racial, gendered, historical, able-bodiedness, etc.) this does not diminish the power that comes with these privileges. And often, *privilege is a blinding constraint.* It is a constraint in the sense that it blocks understanding, empathy, compassion and other ways of seeing the world. Comfort numbs. Certainty obscures. Those who fear losing what they have (including control) also tighten their hold on privilege once they understand that privilege. Self-reflexivity does not necessarily lead to selfless change. Yet, without our privileges, we could not engage in this inquiry in the ways we do.

5. *Paradox of perpetuation* – In the hope of trying to address social issues, we often labour to keep the existing structures in place. A generous interpretation would be that philanthropy believes the alternative (e.g. philanthropic foundations not existing) would have a negative impact on those it is trying to support. A *realpolitik* interpretation of this is that we keep the dominant structures in place because those who benefit from existing systems cannot tolerate what would have to be relinquished through true structural change. That is, most people do not have the psychological and emotional fortitude, selflessness and compassion to imagine a world where the existing structures (and their respective positions in those structures) do not exist. As a result, we perpetuate the existing system and its destructive forces even in the face of annihilation, while discussing systemic change in earnest. Partly this is because we fear the unknown more than we fear our current trajectory, no matter how suicidal the path may be.

6. *Paradox of planning* – Part of the practice of sense-making is to become more *contextually sensitive* in order to become more *contextually relevant* to present, historical and future states. Yet our desire to be more sensitive or relevant does not *necessarily* mean we will be any more successful in understanding future states. The future is, by definition, unknowable, emergent and non-linear. Even invoking the language of transitions or pathways implies that we can somehow plan for a future to come when in fact we are simply planning with the limited knowledge of the future we believe we

hold now. Of course, this is still a worthy endeavour and may increase our ability to better navigate the contours of emerging futures.

7. *Paradox of pronouncement* – Language both matters and is inherently limited. Language can be hegemonic in its application. The dominant culture perpetuates the elevation of the written word. Beyond language, we are engaging in abstract thought and rational arguments to analyse and describe embodied, subjective phenomena. In that sense, embodied cognition and pronouncements of the word are in paradoxical tension. The very act of pronouncement is an act embedded within the dominant culture of capitalist modernity and reinforces dualistic thought.

8. *Paradox of 'post'* – This is related to the paradox above: we use the language of post capitalism throughout this text. As mentioned in the section about post capitalism, the prefix *post* can imply a "context after" but it can also imply a state which is informed by the context prior to it. Both are true. Post capitalism is informed by capitalism but is not an end-state that simply comes after it (which is why we spell the two words separately without a dash). There are simultaneous post capitalist realities that exist right now, some of which have existed for hundreds of years (e.g. various Indigenous cultures) and some for decades (e.g. Zapatistas). Also, an aspect of many lived alternatives to capitalism is to deconstruct the conditioning of future fixation, of a belief that a new society will necessarily be better. As such, we aim to stand in the present, rooted in a deep historical understanding while actively building new-ancient-emerging ways of living, knowing and being beyond the logic of capitalism.

9. *Paradox of performance* – We perform and embody the values of the culture we live in, even if we do not agree with the dominant culture or its tenets (this could also be called the paradox of culture). For example, one key feature of the colonial mindset is a focus on urgency, analysis, planning, and rational action, rather than on being, allowing, and surrendering, perhaps to a deeper and unknowable cosmic design (intelligent or otherwise). Another key feature of the colonial mindset is the belief in its own exceptionalism – setting the exceptional urgency of this moment above all other critical junctures of history through which our species and our planet have passed through. Accordingly, we perform or enact the dominant culture through our grandiose sense of our own agency and influence, all so that we can diagnose

and address systemic problems at a systemic level. And yet, an attempt to deepen our systems-level understanding is critical to contextualising the meta-crisis and our roles within it, and in becoming more self-aware and expansive in our consciousness, regardless of outcomes.

10. *Paradox of perfection* – The coming to form of this text (i.e. publishing a book) implies some kind of neat, tidy end-state. Yet, many of the references and examples we use will already be dated by the time of publishing, and emerging examples will be omitted as the world(s) continues to turn in waves of expansion and entropy. This work is an ongoing exploration of theory and praxis, and we will endeavour to find other ways to deepen this inquiry and share our findings (e.g. in-person gatherings, online discussions, etc.) with this book being simply one output, as a product of its context.

Now that we have made some of our working paradoxes explicit, we will start proceedings with a brief outline of the book, before moving into the broader context in which this inquiry, and all its relevant paradoxes, are embedded.

STRUCTURE OF THE TEXT

~

"He who jumps into the void owes no explanation to those who stand and watch."
- Jean-Luc Godard[47]

"There are no dangerous thoughts for the simple reason that thinking itself is such a dangerous enterprise... Non-thinking is even more dangerous."
- Hannah Arendt[48]

We will gradually proceed towards considering the hopes and perils of dangerous thinking. In order to sufficiently understand philanthropy, let alone gesture towards post capitalist philanthropy, we will first situate our inquiry within four nested hierarchies: the global economic operating system (i.e. capitalism); philanthropy as a by-product of this economic operating system; philanthropic institutions as nodes upholding the dominant logic; and the individuals working within these organisations who are both affected by, and perpetuate, core aspects of the dominant system.

The latter half of the book will go beyond inverting these traditional, command-and-control, nested hierarchies to better understand the interconnected interplay among and between the individual, institution, sector, and operating system through interconnected wholes. We describe this as *spiral logic*.

We start with cosmology, then turn to what individuals as webs of relational entanglements can do to create social ecologies, which can then disrupt the patterning of the larger sector. We will move into the potential roles and archetypes for foundations and introduce a working framework we call the *Five Elements mandala*. We will then discuss the evolving role for the philanthropic sector with the goal of becoming *contextually relevant in troubled times*. We will then conclude with potential pathways for enacting praxis for the inevitable transition(s).

---

[47] Shafto (2006)
[48] Arendt (2013), p. 150

Throughout the book, we offer avenues into other ways of knowing, sensing and being. This includes reflection exercises, additional resources to learn more, and embodied practices. We have also commissioned artwork from three visual artists to complement and interpret the ideas within the text. Throughout the text, there are also visual graphics deployed to help demonstrate the more complex concepts. We include all of these so the reader/viewer/participant can engage with and beyond the written word.

We aim to develop a living praxis for how we can better see our unexamined assumptions and blind-spots, feel into our individual and collective response-abilities, open up to imaginative possibilities and mytho-poetic methods of expression, and honour all those who are dedicated to the service of life, death, and liberation in times of collapse and renewal.

ARTWORK ON FOLLOWING PAGE:
"HUMAN IN THE ANTHROPOCENE:
THE AGE OF CONSEQUENCE"
~ FEDERICO CRUZ ~

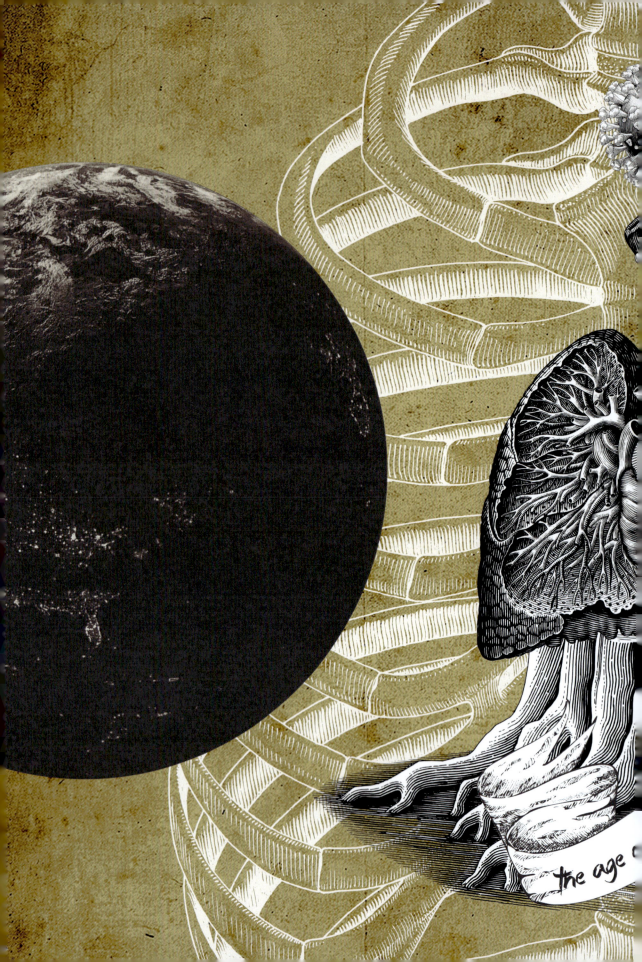

PART ONE
INTO THE PARADOX

INTO THE PARADOX

THE FIRST HIERARCHY

~

GLOBAL NEOLIBERAL OPERATING SYSTEM

"The capitalist system has imposed on us a logic of competition, progress and limitless growth. This regime of production and consumption seeks profit without limits, separating human beings from nature and imposing a logic of domination upon nature, transforming everything into commodities... Humanity confronts a great dilemma: to continue on the path of capitalism, depredation, and death, or to choose the path of harmony with nature and respect for life."

- People's Agreement of Cochabamba[49]

"This structure of modernity has created a feedback loop that starts with fears: a fear of chaos, a fear of loss, a fear of death, a fear of pain, a fear of pointlessness, worthlessness and meaninglessness that then become allocated desires for specific things. So, for example, the fear of scarcity becomes a desire for accumulation. And then these desires, within the modern structures and feedback loops, become entitlements: the desire for accumulation becomes, in turn, a perceived entitlement to property or ownership."

- Vanessa Andreotti[50]

The exponential curve has become a cliché in the 21st century. We are in the midst of the deepest meta-crisis humanity has ever seen – a quickening of ecological collapse;

---

[49] World People's Conference on Climate Change and the Rights of Mother Earth (April 2010)
[50] Andreotti (December 23, 2020)

faster climate feedback loops than predicted; unprecedented human-created species extinction; increasing incidences of pandemics as humans colonise and destroy ever-more of the natural world; increasing divisions of hierarchy leading to even more fascism, racism and xenophobia; spiking inequality and resulting power concentrations with eight billionaires now holding the same amount of wealth as the majority of humanity[51]; and inhumane poverty at a time of peak human material wealth. All of these phenomena are the logical outcomes of our current economic, political and cultural system.

For every dollar of new economic growth since 2008, about 93 cents ends up in the hands of the top 1%.[52] And only about 5 cents of that dollar ends up in the hands of the world's majority – 60% of humanity.[53] Therefore, by definition, wealth creation actively creates inequality and poverty.

At the same time, the current economic orthodoxy states that we must grow the global economy at 3% a year to avoid stagnation and/or recession. The basic assumption underpinning this is that within a growth/debt system, our growth rate has to exceed our interest rates in order for debt to be paid back, and therefore, for money to remain valuable. Three percent annual growth may not sound like much, but because it is an exponential function, it requires a doubling of the global economy every 23 years.[54]

Let's give a concrete example. The global economy grew roughly 2.6% between 2018 and 2019, generating an additional $1.3T worth of products and services.[55] In other words, commodified natural resources and commodified human labour grew in assigned economic value to the tune of $1.3T, which is a small number compared to previous years of global growth. However, this $1.3T is the equivalent of the total global GDP in 1960. It took us from the dawn of humanity to 1960 to achieve an annual GDP of $1.3T and we now require that amount of growth just in the delta, the additional growth, to be *added every year*. Next year we may need to grow by 1970's GDP, then 1990's, etc. Soon we'll need to grow by the magnitude of 2022's GDP in order for the global Ponzi scheme not to implode upon itself.

---

[51] Francis (2020), pp. 490-498
[52] Robinson, P. (2012)
[53] Woodward (2015)
[54] Hickel (July 16, 2018)
[55] World Bank. Current GDP (USD) Calculator (2021)

We have already crossed six of the nine planetary boundaries (including climate change, biodiversity loss, land-use change, biogeochemical flows, chemical pollution and fresh water change) and we are already in the midst of the Sixth Mass Extinction with over 200 species a day going extinct, a thousand times the baseline rate of extinction.[56] How could we even fathom continuing to grow the global economy at 3% a year and consuming the way we currently do? What is the ideology at the root of the civilisational cancer of growth?

The short answer is capitalism. In other words, a system that is organised around extracting and accumulating surplus value, and then reinvesting that capital for increased expansion through ever-more exploitation of human labour and the natural world. Of course, capitalism is not a static system. It is constantly morphing and mutating. In the 1980s, the dominant form of capitalism became *neoliberalism* – an accelerated, globalised incarnation that purposefully deregulated the global economy, cheapened labour and expanded corporate control to keep the engine of growth going.

Some have argued that we have surpassed the era of neoliberalism. For example, former Greek Finance Minister Yanis Varoufakis has argued that we now live within an empire of techno-feudalism which entails a monopolistic control of privatised space managed by global technology giants like Google and Meta.[57] Although this may be true in certain spatial dimensions, such as the technosphere and emerging "metaverse", the dominant global system in terms of the global supply chain of goods & services, government policy, popular culture, the NGO industrial complex, corporate decision-making and, indeed, philanthropy are all still plainly embedded in the logic of neoliberalism.

As such, for the context and purpose of this text, we will use neoliberalism as the descriptor for the global economic operating system, as it is currently the paramount ideology that is the heir to proto-capitalism, industrial capitalism, colonialism, imperialism and other forms of organised extraction that have progressed to this current moment of the meta-crisis. We will also use the terms *late-stage capitalism* and *capitalist modernity* interchangeably with neoliberalism, although the former highlights the extreme nature of capitalism before collapse and the latter incorporates

---

[56] See Rockström, Will, Noone, Persson, Chapin, Lambin, Lenton. et al. (2009) and Wang-Erlandsson, Tobian, Van der Ent, Fetzer, Te Wierik, Porkka, Staal, et al. (2022, April 26).
[57] Varoufakis (June 28, 2021)

a critique of rationalism, materialism, positivism, hegemonic notions of progress and development, as well as other aspects of modernity.

Think of neoliberalism as a snowball still gathering heft and momentum from a five-thousand year progression into ever more complex forms of hierarchy, patriarchy, monoculture, abstraction, ecocide and alienation. Every time we have chosen the expansion of capital over the living inputs in each accretion of capital, we helped expand the neoliberal snowball – even if we did so with the well-intentioned belief that the accretion of capital would support life in the long-run. As Immanuel Wallerstein eloquently states in *Historical Capitalism*: "Whenever, over time, it was the accumulation of capital that regularly took priority over alternative objectives, we are justified in saying that we are observing a capitalist system in operation."[58]

> *Of course, capitalism is not a static system. It is constantly morphing and mutating. In the 1980s, the dominant form of capitalism became neoliberalism – an accelerated, globalised incarnation that purposefully deregulated the global economy, cheapened labour and expanded corporate control to keep the engine of growth going.*

We do not state this in order to make an ideological or political statement, or to repeat information you may already know. If you feel well-familiarised with this topic, feel free to skip to Part II. Our aim in starting with neoliberalism is to create a shared language and a starting point to situate philanthropy within the ideology and theology from whence it came.

We ask the reader to practise *embodied cognition* where you feel how and where the ideas of the dominant culture may live within or react in your body. There have been hundreds of books and academic articles written about this topic. Our aim is not to create an exhaustive list or to assume we know how to best synthesise this information. Rather, we are introducing the major through-lines of neoliberalism as we subjectively see them, as they hold relevance and bearing to philanthropy, and how they are programmed within all of our somatic landscapes.

---

[58] Wallerstein (2014), p.13

NESTED HIERARCHIES OF DOMINANT PHILANTHROPY

Number of People Affected

GLOBAL NEOLIBERAL OPERATING SYSTEM

PHILANTHROPY AS EXTENSION AND EXTERNALITY

INSTITUTIONS AS FRACTAL NODES

INDIVIDUALS AS REPLICATORS

The dominant global ideology of neoliberalism has at least five major philosophical tenets.

From the Enlightenment onwards, a core tenet of Western thought – which has been super-charged by neoliberalism – is that human beings are inherently egoistic and competitive by nature. This "human nature" defines our relationship to other beings through a competitive lens (e.g. am I better, richer, etc.). This worldview was mainstreamed through the logic derived from selective half-truths about the Darwinian theory of natural selection, the philosophies of David Hume and Thomas Hobbes, and the political economy of Adam Smith.[59] Essentially, the belief dictates that we are all engaged in a battle for survival with other aggressive, survivalist humans who are "red in tooth and claw".[60]

The second is the belief that hierarchy is inevitable and, in fact, important for order. Without clear hierarchy and rule of law, society would descend into "mere anarchy" or a Hobbesian state of war. This belief justifies the nation-state, governments, war, taxation, constitutions and other laws. The ordering of this hierarchy is also sustained and perpetuated, as determined by God, genetics and superiority. The white male rests at the top of this hierarchy, embedded within a *manifest destiny* and supremacy as the "natural order" of the world.

The third tenet is that the individual is the primary unit of power. As Margaret Thatcher, one of the key architects of neoliberalism summed it up: "…there's no such thing as society. There are individual men and women and there are families. And no government can do anything except through people, and people must look after themselves first."[61]

The fourth pillar of neoliberalism is that material comfort, wealth and power equate to well-being, meaning, and life success – which are then equated to virtue. Therefore, rich people and powerful institutions are good, while poor or disenfranchised people are bad, lazy, irresponsible, inept or just need more 'personal opportunities'.

---

[59] In Adam Smith's *Theory of Moral Sentiments*, he often laments the ills of what he calls "commercial society." For a good introduction, see Rasmussen (June 9, 2016).

[60] This phrase was first used to describe nature in Alfred Lord Tennyson's poem *In Memoriam A. H. H.* from 1850 and is often used as a justification for capitalist beliefs on human nature. See Tennyson (2013), p.1166.

[61] Thatcher (September 23, 1987)

As such, what is prioritised is the offering of more wealth creation or power accumulation opportunities for individuals, rather than the task of designing systems for individual and collective well-being across multiple dimensions (material and non-material). The 'white man's burden' thus continues in the form of economic development of the so-called Third World. We have re-interpreted material poverty and powerlessness as moral failings of individuals that can be corrected by wealthier, more entrepreneurial, more institutionally resourced people.

What is critical here – and entangled with the last two pillars – is the perceived nature of neoliberalism as *ahistorical*; there is virtually no historical perspective on how wealth was created or acquired. There is rarely an acknowledgement of the drivers of historical wealth creation, including colonialism, enslavement, genocide, patriarchy, imperialism, perpetual war, pillage and "accumulation by dispossession".[62] Rather, the individual must pull themselves up by their bootstraps much like the descendants of the vanquishers around them, and aspire to find meaning in their same extractive, consumerist ways of living and being.

Finally, the metaphysical aspect of neoliberalism states that separation from the natural world and materialism (i.e. that the world is made of fixed, separate material objects) define our relationship to the "outside". We are separate, atomised beings battling Nature itself with the aim of conquest and domination. We ourselves are dualistically split between mind and body, our advanced, God-like nature and our mere physical shell. All of our interactions with the material world can be understood rationally through our unique and advanced minds. *Homo economicus*, the rational man, is the pinnacle of the human ideal, and therefore the pinnacle of all Life. As Descartes infamously stated: "I think therefore I am" (*cogito ergo sum*).[63]

This original separation between humans and nature was deeply rooted in the invention of dualist thought. As Raj Patel and Jason Moore have argued, the emergence of dualist thought in the 16th and 17th centuries was purposely pursued because early capitalists knew they had to destroy animist perspectives, as these worldviews posed obstacles to the kinds of exploitation of nature and life that capitalism requires. Nature had to be seen as a collection of inanimate objects to be used, and Indigenous peoples and African slaves had to be seen as less than

---

[62] Harvey (2005), p.283
[63] Descartes (2013), p.17

human, in order for continued pillage and destruction to be culturally accepted.[64] The Valladolid debate in 1550 is considered the first moral debate about colonialism, where European thinkers started to work out the ideas to provide an ontological justification for their ongoing imperialist exploits of "the New World".[65]

This happened alongside the introduction of the printing press instigating a triumph of written, symbolic language, and eventually the construction of rationality as being superior to oral and communal traditions, and other ways of knowing more broadly. This also gave control to those who determined which languages would be written and who would be literate, and therefore rational enough to be considered civilised and human.[66]

Neoliberalism can be summarised in this equation:

Selfishness is rational
Rationality determines reality;
Therefore selfishness is fundamental to reality.[67]

> ... the metaphysical aspect of neoliberalism states that separation from the natural world and materialism (i.e. that the world is made of fixed, separate material objects) define our relationship to the "outside". We are separate, atomised beings battling Nature itself with the aim of conquest and domination. We ourselves are dualistically split between mind and body, our advanced, God-like nature and our mere physical shell.

---

[64] Patel & Moore (2018)
[65] We are grateful to Jason Hickel for this insight. For further details about the Vallaloid debate, see Daher (2021).
[66] See Anderson (2006) and Shlain (1998).
[67] Some of these initial arguments that we have built on were developed in a two-part series entitled "Capitalism is just a story and other dangerous thoughts". See Ladha & Kirk (2015).

SUMMARY OF NEO-LIBERAL PREMISES

I.
Humans are inherently selfish and competitive.

II.
Hierarchy is inevitable, and in fact, necessary for order.

III.
The individual is the primary unit of power.

IV.
Material wealth and power determine well-being, meaning, life success and virtue.

V.
Separation and materialism define our relationship with the world; and this reality can be understood rationally.

> *We recommend that you keep a journal for the exercises and reflection questions as you go through the text.*

REFLECTION EXERCISE:
NEO-LIBERAL PREMISES

. . .

Selfishness is rational

Rationality determines reality;

Therefore selfishness is fundamental to reality.

- PAUSE -

As you read the summary of the premises on the opposite page, please notice any feelings or sensations that arise in your body. Notice the quality of your mind. For example, are you arguing internally, debating whether this is true or not, noting where you agree or disagree, searching for how this is relevant to you? Notice where in your body each sensation lies and if you can name the thought-form that exists (e.g. anger, annoyance, harmony, resonance, acceptance, resistance, etc.).

Now go back and reflect on each tenet of neoliberalism *one by one.*

. . .

Consider the following questions with as much specificity as possible:

How do the core tenets of neoliberalism play out in your day-to-day life? In your workplace; the organisations you interact with; your understanding of the role of government; your ways of engaging with family, community and society more broadly?

Where do you notice these beliefs playing out in your interpersonal dynamics with others?

How do these tenets play out in your body? Where do they live?

How do these tenets shape the way you see and prepare for the future?

What are the ways in which you uphold or resist each tenet?

Over the next few days, find examples of where and how these premises show up in your interactions, reading the news, and engagement in social media (if you partake in such activities; no judgement).

Note these and any other insights that come in your reflections.

. . .

It almost goes without saying (but we will anyway) the implications for this ideology are insidious and life-destroying. The dominant worldview of neoliberalism creates a moral hierarchy by which human beings, and a particular subset thereof (i.e. the white male), are at the pinnacle, separating humanity from each other and from the natural world in which we are enmeshed.

Neoliberalism erases the history of extreme violence, forced colonisation, imperialist wars, genocide, rape and pillage that ushered in the current inequities and hierarchies. It ignores the trauma our ancestors endured and that our bodies continue to experience and carry, whether they were perpetrators or victims. It diminishes the felt experiences of the world's majority. It gives structural power to white supremacy, as the descendants of Western Europeans acquired a 500-year headstart on capital accumulation, enshrining a perceived correlation with wealth, status, success and race. Relatedly, there is a fetishisation of what Resmaa Menakem, a contemporary scholar and therapist, calls "white-body supremacy", the notion that the white body is the arbiter of normality by which all other bodies are judged.[68]

Neoliberalism leads directly to the economics of the self-obsessed individual, which leads to the atomisation of society and the focus on personal consumption as salvation. Here, even our traumas or societal injustices are our own faults and our own responsibilities. We have to 'invest more' into ourselves through a growing, multi-billion-dollar self-care marketplace.

Neoliberalism justifies the bankrupt notion of trickle-down economics, smuggling in notions such as: "self-interest benefits everyone", "there's an all-knowing invisible hand", "there is supreme efficiency in the market", "rich people create jobs for everyone", and other selective half-truths. These are the core alibis for land-grabbing and tax evasion amongst corporations and the world's power elite, all of which are, of course, directly related to philanthropy.

This also leads to the continued colonisation and pillaging of "sacrifice zones" which encompass most of the global South.[69] When it comes to climate change, high-income countries are the primary drivers of ecological breakdown. Research by Jason Hickel shows that: "The global North is responsible for 92 percent of emissions

---

[68] Menakem (2017)
[69] Manji (2019)

in excess of the planetary boundary, while the consequences of climate breakdown fall disproportionately upon the global South. The South already suffers the vast majority of the damage inflicted by climate breakdown, and if temperatures exceed 1.5 degrees centigrade, much of the tropics could experience heat events that exceed the limits of human survival."[70]

> *Neoliberalism erases the history of extreme violence, forced colonisation, imperialist wars, genocide, rape and pillage that ushered in the current inequities and hierarchies. It ignores the trauma our ancestors endured and that our bodies continue to experience and carry, whether they were perpetrators or victims. It diminishes the felt experiences of the world's majority. It gives structural power to white supremacy, as the descendants of Western Europeans acquired a 500-year headstart on capital accumulation, enshrining a perceived correlation with wealth, status, success and race.*

Hickel reminds us: "Crucially, these high levels of consumption depend on a significant net appropriation from the global South through unequal exchange, including 10.1 billion tons of embodied raw materials and 379 billion hours of embodied labour per year."[71] In other words, economic growth in the geopolitical global North relies on continued colonisation of the geopolitical South, the appropriation of the atmosphere, and the extraction of Southern resources and labour.[72]

Moreover, neoliberalism elevates the liberal democratic state to the apex of human civilization, perpetuating elitism, inequality and a form of democracy that is based on a governing leisure class. Gopal Dayaneni, from the Oakland-based educational think-tank and activist collective *Movement Generation*, elaborates on this point:

---

[70] Hickel (2020), p.115

[71] Hickel (2021), p.1

[72] We are grateful to Marai Larasi for reminding us of the distinction between a geopolitical North and South, rather than simply validating the inherent hegemony of geographic location. For example, Australia and New Zealand are in the geographic South but are industrialised, capitalist-colonialist nation-states.

"The nature of democracy is that we have inherited it from slavery. I don't mean American slavery. I mean Greco-Roman slavery. Even the notion of the Senate, the idea that there was enough surplus generated through the extraction of wealth from other people's labour and the labour of the living world, that a group of people can govern as a form of recreation abstracted from daily life. That's the nature of representative democracy. It can only exist through the mass exploitation of labour and the living world."[73]

We have taken one form of governance and elevated it to the global standard, replicating injustices and inequities under the guise of liberal democracy. The merger of neoliberalism and representative democracy has created a government-corporate complex that perpetuates and exacerbates the major aspects of our meta-crisis while purporting to be the only solution.

The concentration of wealth and power then further undermines democracy through the phenomenon that is described in the United States simply as "money in politics" (i.e. the ability for corporations to lobby for more favourable outcomes, further exacerbating economic and social inequity in an ever-growing feedback loop).

Relatedly, neoliberalism prioritises private property over collective wealth and well-being, which in turn leads to what the late Harvard economist J.K. Galbraith described as "private affluence and public squalor" – manifesting in privatised benefits but socialised costs. This is not an externality, or unintended consequence, of capitalism.[74] The enclosure of the commons was a deliberate strategy and process that power elites architected from the 16th century onwards. Enclosure was the process of "internal colonisation", and colonisation is a process of enclosure.[75]

Critically, neoliberalism elevates the growth of economic activity, measured by Gross Domestic Product, as the primary goal of civilisation. To quote Hickel again: "What makes capitalism distinctive isn't that it has markets, but that it is organised around perpetual growth. It is a system that pulls ever-expanding quantities of nature and human labour into circuits of accumulation. And it works according to a simple, straightforward formula: take more than you give back."[76]

---

[73] Dayaneni (November 19, 2021)
[74] Galbraith (2007), p.16
[75] Hickel (2020), p.54
[76] Hickel (2020), p.41

By and large, the dominant culture has no meaningful cosmology or metaphysical purpose beyond consuming, exploiting, and producing more monetised material output within a transactional, extractive system. Time is an arrow, and the march of progress is ever upwards – validated by the fact that "we now have a microwave in every house" (to paraphrase Steven Pinker[77]), even as the intrinsic, relational bonds of the household and community are frayed. This is the epitome (and the caricature) of the Davos worldview.

Neoliberalism is more akin to a theology than an economic ideology. It provides answers to the major inquiries or *first principles* of an institutional religion including:

- **Ontology** – Selfishness and competition are our human nature, and this nature can only be regulated by a God-like invisible hand.

- **Epistemology** – Humans are masters of the material world, mediated by rational thought, in an upward march towards "progress".

- **Ethics** – The pursuit of self-interest, market growth and economic maximisation is the goal of individuals and society.

- **Cosmology** – Humans are entitled to extract and conquer the natural world and other beings.

- **Metaphysics** – Humans are distinctly separate from the natural world and inherently special.

- **Aesthetics** – The human, especially the white male, holds the "objective gaze" of reality and beauty.

- **Political philosophy** – Hierarchically organised capitalist nation-states that compete through economic growth are the most ideal and efficient models to organise society.

---

[77] Pinker (2011)

Although we may feel that we intellectually understand most of these implications, the deeper truth is that there is now an invisible hand that lives within all of us, and most of us have accepted and integrated this apparent reality. The phenomenon of the all-encompassing, internalised ideology has been described as "capitalist realism" by the late political philosopher Mark Fisher. We are enmeshed in a world in which we cannot see ourselves outside of the capitalist system nor can we even imagine it as an alternative to our existence.[78]

The economic historian Immanuel Wallerstein describes the process of this acculturation through the imposition of universalism, i.e. how everyone interacts with capitalism in the same ways. He states: "The belief in universalism has been the keystone of the ideological arch of historical capitalism. Universalism is a faith, as well as an epistemology. It requires not merely respect but reverence for the elusive but allegedly real phenomenon of truth."[79]

The totalitarian colonisation and universalisation of the neoliberal worldview as 'Truth' is manifest in the sectors of the *body politic* as well as in the cells of our physical bodies. In their powerful book *Inflamed: Deep Medicine and the Anatomy of Injustice*, Dr. Rupa Mayra and Raj Patel highlight the interconnections among the trinity of colonialism, white supremacy and capitalism, and the traumatic and inflammatory effects on the body, soil, and the broader ecology.[80]

The ongoing neoliberal exploitation of humans and the natural world intensifies trauma, thereby weakening our individual and collective ability to regulate and respond (i.e. with commensurate life-force), while destroying the ecosystems on which Life depends, further reinforcing the cycle of violence. Hence, neoliberalism is both a structural driver of trauma and its largest beneficiary. It feeds and is fed by trauma. One could argue that neoliberalism is the violent god of trauma incarnate.

---

[78] See Fisher (2009) for a cogent unpacking of the totalising effect of global capitalism.
[79] Wallerstein (2014), p.98
[80] Marya & Patel (2021)

Neoliberalism is also the source code from which institutional philanthropy is born and continues to constitute itself. This is the theatrical stage on which philanthropy appears. As we will later discuss in detail, philanthropy performs acts of (self-appointed) saviourhood through strategic benevolence while never truly acknowledging or addressing how we ended up performing and/or watching the tragi-comedy (i.e. the meta-crisis) in the first place. As one funder-activist said to us: "As a funder I sometimes feel as if I'm participating in Groundhog Day – a perpetually looping version of a Greek tragedy, where everyone already knows not only the story but also the final outcome – while continuing to carry on in exactly the same way."[81]

> *Hence, neoliberalism is both a structural driver of trauma and its largest beneficiary. It feeds and is fed by trauma. One could argue that neoliberalism is the violent god of trauma incarnate.*

[81] Lipman (January 21, 2022)

INTO THE PARADOX

ARTWORK ON FOLLOWING PAGE:
"THE BUREAUCRACY OF BEING"
~ FEDERICO CRUZ ~

REFLECTION EXERCISE:
NEOLIBERALISM AS THEOLOGY

...

Of these key phrases, which are the two or three concepts that are most striking to you? In your own life, how do they connect to and reinforce the dominant paradigm?

- HUMAN EXCEPTIONALISM
- AHISTORICAL WORLDVIEW
- WHITE SUPREMACY
- SEPARATION FROM THE NATURAL WORLD
- HYPER-INDIVIDUALISM
- ELEVATION OF SCIENTIFIC MATERIALISM
- CONSOLIDATION OF GOVERNMENT-CORPORATE POWER
- ECONOMIC GROWTH AS THE CIVILIZATIONAL PRIME DIRECTIVE
- INVISIBLE HAND AS AN INFALLIBLE DEITY
- PRIVATE PROPERTY OVER COLLECTIVE WEALTH
- PHILANTHROPY AS A SAVIOUR

THE SECOND HIERARCHY

~

PHILANTHROPY AS EXTENSION AND EXTERNALITY OF NEOLIBERALISM

"We would like to create a world where we are not being exploited and where we do not have to exploit anyone else."

- Vinoba Bhave[82]

"Having wealth is unjustified, but the Rockefellers justify it by doing good. I had to cut through all this and understand that there is no rational justification for my family having the amount of money that it has, and that the only honest thing to say in defence of it is that we like having the money and the present social system allows us to keep it."

- Steven Rockefeller, 1983[83]

As we come to better understand the dominant culture and political economy in which we are all embedded, we can start to see the role of philanthropy as both an extension and externalisation of capitalism. At best, institutional philanthropy serves as the prophylactic sector to capitalism in the sense that it tries to ensure that the worst abuses of the market system are softened through an arbitrary and elite-controlled "redistribution" of a relatively small portion of accumulated wealth. This of course achieves the intended objective of having an *insignificant but conspicuous impact*. As one interviewee, an elder statesman in the philanthropic space remarked: "Philanthropy has done some good but has never really done anything great".[84]

Philanthropy is also a vehicle for further tax-free wealth accumulation and the perpetuation of unjust systems through public perception management and a vector for unchecked influence upon governments and persuasion over civil society to ensure the values of the dominant culture and power-elite remain intact, and even

---

[82] Srivastava (1967), pp. 206
[83] Kashtan, (November 25, 2016)
[84] Knight (September 28, 2021)

represented, within the machinations of reform. The obvious example that comes to mind is the Gates Foundation's enormous influence on the United Nations, often leading the UN and its various agencies to change policies in favour of both Gates Foundation and Microsoft interests.[85]

One of the deepest contradictions of neoliberalism is that a smaller and smaller group of people have become the largest beneficiary of the long arc of historical pillage. In the dominant culture these people are often perceived merely as 'winners'. As a result of this economic head start, to continue the neoliberal metaphor of 'the game', the power elites then created philanthropic foundations to expand the playing field – i.e. to use the perpetual existence and tax-free growth of this accumulated wealth in order to determine how and in what way civil society and social movements can work, live, organise and spend their time.[86]

The vast majority of philanthropic dollars have also come from corporations, as the growing state-corporate nexus further concentrates wealth. In 2015, 69 of the 100 largest global economic entities on Earth were corporations, with the corporate sector representing a clear majority over countries.[87] The revenues of Royal Dutch Shell, for instance, were greater than the GDP of Norway and dwarfed the GDP of Thailand, Denmark and South Africa.[88]

In other words, more economic power is in private hands than public. Many of the dominant corporations in our world started the globalisation process by exploiting human labour where it was cheapest and where the rules were the most slack. They then capitalised on the lack of global governance around tax and opted out of the social contract with the rest of humanity. There is presently up to 32 trillion dollars sitting in tax havens[89], and 60% of world trade happens between multinational corporations' own subsidiaries, largely through what's known as transfer mis-pricing (i.e. selling goods and services to themselves, largely at a loss, to counter revenue gains in which they would have to pay tax).[90]

---

[85] Seitz & Martens (2017), pp. 46-50
[86] Giridharadas (2018)
[87] Global Justice Now (September 12, 2016)
[88] Global Justice Now (2015)
[89] See Tax Justice Network FAQs
[90] Shaxson (2011)

And then there's the kicker: corporations often actively subvert democracy to further entrench their power and wealth. Research from Harvard's *Safra Center for Ethics* shows that corporations receive up to $220 return on investment for every dollar invested in lobbying the United States Congress.[91] This type of corporate subterfuge pays in various degrees in other contexts as well. Under these conditions, why would a corporation 'invest' their money in anything else?

The connections between corporations, tax evasion, human/planetary exploitation, lobbying and philanthropy are intricate and intimate. In many countries, starting from the United States, any individual or corporation that makes a philanthropic donation receives a direct tax break on the funding amount against their income. So philanthropy is often used as part of a larger tax minimisation strategy, further concentrating wealth. A recent investigative report by *The Nation* magazine concluded that Bill Gates has personally received more money back in the form of personal tax breaks than he has given in philanthropic grants through the activities of the Gates Foundation.[92]

The result of this mix of tax avoidance, offshore money laundering, transfer mispricing, corporate shell games, and charity tax exemptions is that the top 1% pays virtually no tax. Recent research by the journalist think-tank *ProPublica*, using a trove of leaked IRS tax returns, showed that the effective tax rate for the ultra-rich is almost non-existent. For example, from 2014 to 2018 Warren Buffett's effective tax rate on his wealth was 0.1%; Jeff Bezos's was 0.98%; Michael Bloomberg's was 1.3%; and Elon Musk's was 3.3%. The investigative researchers paint the backdrop for these statistics: "Many Americans live paycheck to paycheck, amassing little wealth and paying the federal government a percentage of their income that rises if they earn more. In recent years, the median American household earned about $70,000 annually and paid 14% in federal taxes."[93]

Then there are also new and emerging vehicles for further extraction and obfuscation. One of the most seductively pernicious is the donor-advised fund (DAF), which is also one of the fastest growing segments of philanthropy. DAF's allow funders to make grants to fund vehicles (even with total anonymity) while fully receiving

---

[91] Lessig (2011), p.117
[92] Schwab (March 17, 2020)
[93] Eisinger, Ernsthausen & Kiel (June 8, 2021)

immediate tax benefits of charitable giving (even though the distributions to actual charities and nonprofits may not occur for years to come).[94] For example, MacKenzie Scott, who is one of the largest DAF donors – has given away billions of dollars and has been celebrated over the past couple of years for the size, type and speed of her grants – made far more money in 2021 than she gave away.[95]

There is also another pernicious mechanism in this regard: the grantor retained annuity trust (GRAT), which allows funds to move assets from private corporations to family trusts without tax implications. Recent research, ironically from Bloomberg News, shows how Phil Knight, the founder of Nike, is using GRATs to transfer huge sums of wealth to his children without paying inheritance tax.[96]

In an interview with the authors, Colin Greer, a long-time philanthropic practitioner and the president of the *New World Foundation* (a progressive funder based in New York), defined philanthropy as *money thrice stolen*: "The money is first stolen through the unfair, rigged lottery of cut-throat neoliberalism. Then it is stolen again by redirecting public money through significant tax breaks, supporting the ongoing expansion of the initial endowments which are largely invested in the very same extractive system. Then finally, these funds are 'morally cleansed' when a small portion of the funds go through the public enactment of supporting civil society, energetically, reputationally and physically extracting once more from the fabric of society to confer more power, intelligence, goodness, magnanimity, etc. upon the benevolent benefactors."[97] All the while, there is a steady imposition of conservative values, cultural tropes, mores, and norms on the grantees – those distant practitioners who must fit into philanthropic siloes and interest areas and undergo tedious applications, milestone reports, and other funder-imposed requirements, to create a "theatre of effective philanthropy" and to maintain good funder-grantee relations.

In 2018, philanthropy as a sector represented a $1.5T dollar industry globally.[98] This accounted for roughly 1.7% of global GDP that year. That is roughly the size of a

---

[94] In 2020, the total charitable assets held in donor-advised funds grew to $159.8 billion, nearly a 10% increase over 2019. See Theis (November 9, 2021).

[95] Hartmans (August 6, 2021)

[96] Steverman, Melin & Pendleton (October 21, 2021)

[97] Greer (June 17, 2021). For transparency's sake, the *New World Foundation* is the fiscal sponsor of the *Transition Resource Circle*.

[98] Johnson (2018)

major G7 country like Canada.[99] Indeed, there is virtually no major social issue or social movement in the world that can operate outside of the "charitable-industrial complex"[100] funded by big philanthropy, unless of course, it is volunteer-run and does not require capital. And so, by design, social justice movements are constrained, in terms of content and form, and are existentially challenged in a David versus Goliath battle where capital will only feed what ultimately serves the interests of capital. Philanthropy is incentivised to create a relational structure of dependency and co-optation to increase its mandate of control, ostensibly for public good, and often, is motivated by proximity to socially relevant activists and not-for-profits.

Here it is important to note that we do not believe that philanthropy is some kind of dark-room conspiracy. From the survival of the most basic cell, all the way up to the complexity of an ecosystem, this is how *complex adaptive systems* behave. They create and emerge from matrices of energy and matter that support their existence. The logic of capital is merely the logic of a particular complex, adaptive system. As Thomas Piketty has shown in such detail, left to its own devices, the system will always reward capital with more capital.[101]

The sole priority of complex, adaptive, evolutionary systems is to survive. Once a network becomes sufficiently complex, it becomes self-organising and self-preserving. One way the global economic system preserves itself is to draw into positions of influence those people who best serve its purpose. A capitalist system, whose prime directive is the production of more capital, will work constantly to refine and improve its ability to do just that.

This is where we arrive at the structure of modern philanthropy: *the 5% rule*. In the US, the Tax Reform Act was put into place in 1969, paving the way for the inclusion of the 5% giving threshold in 1976, by which the lobbying machinery of the Rockefellers, Carnegies and other industrialists helped produce the United States IRS code of the 501(C)3 act for tax-exempt status.[102] This has been exported around the world and continues to be promoted as the global model for philanthropy.

---

[99] In 2018, Canada represented roughly 2% of global GDP. For a visual breakdown, see Desjardins (September 10, 2019).
[100] Buffett, P. (July 26, 2013)
[101] Piketty (2014)
[102] United States Congress (1975-1976)

> *In 2018, philanthropy as a sector represented a $1.5T dollar industry globally. This accounted for roughly 1.7% of global GDP that year. That is roughly the size of a major G7 country like Canada. Indeed, there is virtually no major social issue or social movement in the world that can operate outside of the "charitable-industrial complex" funded by big philanthropy, unless of course, it is volunteer-run and does not require capital. And so, by design, social justice movements are constrained, in terms of content and form, and are existentially challenged in a David versus Goliath battle where capital will only feed what ultimately serves the interests of capital.*

What the 5% *rule* means in practice is that a charitable foundation has to give annually a minimum of 5% of its overall endowment in the form of grants or program-related investments. As a result, some foundations give much less than 5% due to 'investment' into these program-related areas which count towards the payout requirement. In practice, the 5% *rule* has effectively become the *ceiling* for giving rather than the *floor*. The other 95% is then treated as tax-exempt investment money.

As long as the funds stay within the confines of foundation activity, the proceeds are not taxed, but rather, sheltered within the entity. These endowment funds are used as untaxed investment capital that is funnelled into the usual engines of capital return: stock markets, bonds, real-estate, fossil fuel companies, etc., which in most cases result in annual returns of more than 5%, creating further, perpetual accumulation. The 5% that is given is removed from the taxable income of the funder, providing a further tax incentive.

Let's break this down further. In 2020, the average rate-of-return for foundation endowments was 13.1%.[103] If we take a $100M foundation as an example, it would be required to give away $5M over the course of the year, but its endowment would have grown to $113M minus $5M for a year end sum of $108M. The following year, this expanded pie of $108M would become $122M (13.1% growth on $108M) minus roughly $5.4M it would give away for a total of roughly $117M. And so the math goes.

---

[103] The NonProfit Times (September 7, 2021)

It does not take an accountant or economist to understand the implications of this model. The extractive-based capital market system and the donors are the two prime beneficiaries. Only a fraction of tax-exempt philanthropic funding is actually used to address social issues while the majority is reinvested in life-destroying activities via the capitalist market with high returns-on-investment. As one interviewee quipped: "Most foundations are hedge funds with a small charitable arm attached on the side."[104] One trustee of a foundation described foundations as: "Mainly private wealth management firms for white people, with side marketing arms focused on dressing up tax avoidance strategies in so-called public and community-spiritedness."[105]

Most philanthropic endowments are heavily invested in the destruction and commodification of the natural world – activities which require increasing amounts of fossil fuels, exploited labour and other living systems to prop up the extraction machine. Then, with a small fraction of its funds, philanthropy doles out grants to not-for-profits (mainly elite private schools, religious institutions, high-status arts institutions, hospitals and universities), and an even smaller fraction to activists whose values the foundation itself has the moral gumption to deem "aligned".

William Jewett Tucker, one of Andrew Carnegie's greatest contemporary critics, once stated: "There is no greater mistake … than that of trying to make charity do the work of justice".[106] Institutional philanthropy not only ignores this sage counsel, but has enshrined and concretised the warning's outcome.

Charity has thus become the alibi for perpetuating injustice. Each individual foundation carves out its roles, its niche, its place in the competitive puzzle of "solving social problems" that capital extraction created in the first place. Throughout the process, philanthropy then replicates and elevates the power dynamics, privileges, status-orientation, and corporate accoutrements of the dominant culture of neoliberalism.

---

[104] Anonymous. (June 14, 2021)
[105] Anonymous. (February 7, 2021)
[106] Vallely (2020), p.629

As Edgar Villanueva, a philanthropist himself, states in *Decolonizing Wealth*:

Far too often, it creates (we create) division and suffering rather than progress and healing.
It is (we are) a sleepwalking sector, white zombies spewing the money of dead white people in the name of charity and benevolence.
It is (we are) colonialism in the empire's newest clothes.
It is (we are) racism in institutional form.

Philanthropy moves at a glacial pace. Epidemics and storms hit, communities go under water literally and metaphorically, Black and brown children get shot dead or lose their youth inside jail cells, families are separated across continents, women are abused and beaten and raped, all of Rome burns while we fiddle with another survey on strategies, another study on impact.[107]

We could go on. Probably, you could as well. Rather, let's do a brief detour into the history of philanthropy to better understand the historical precedents. Feel free to skip this section if you are sufficiently disillusioned.

---

[107] Villanueva (2021), pp. 22-23

A BRIEF DETOUR INTO THE HISTORY OF PHILANTHROPY

The first time the term "philanthropy" is referenced in literature is in the Greek myth of *Prometheus Bound*.[108] Prometheus, a divine god, shares fire with humans. The other gods punish Prometheus with an eternity of torture for sharing divine knowledge with "mere mortals", despite Prometheus' pleas about his love for humanity. This is then the germ concept for bequeathing wealth to the weak and needy, and, in turn, deifying the benevolence of the giver.

The term is resurrected during the creation of the Abrahamic myths. It was rooted in a deep mutuality through the notion of almsgiving – to give and take care of God's children who are without. The idea of philanthropy asked that all creatures should share in God's gifts and creation. Whereas the Greeks did not see a moral requirement for philanthropy, almsgiving was seen as a moral exercise of social justice.

The Judeo-Christian notions of philanthropy were key drivers in the societal Debt Jubilees that were enacted every seven years, where all personal debts were forgiven to restore the cycle of mutuality, altruism and reciprocity.[109] However, the giving away of divine wealth also carried hierarchical order and righteousness, and offered purification to the giver – it became a way to pay indulgences for committed sins.[110] It also reified the giver as superior. Jesus' famous line comes to mind: *"It is more blessed to give than to receive."*[111] This was translated into the infamous Christian dictum, *the hand of the giver is always on top.*

This form of philanthropy was still rooted in an inherent benevolence and tribal mutuality, and in ordinary people playing the contextual role of philanthropist. In sixteenth-century England, giving to your local church became mandatory for the sake of quelling dissent and redistributing wealth. Of course, the backdrop of this was the infamous *Poor Laws* where the English state and elites gave themselves licence to incarcerate and execute vagrants and enclose the commons, removing the ability of the majority to access an autonomous livelihood.

---

[108] Vallely (2020), p.18
[109] Graeber (2012)
[110] Vallely (2020)
[111] Acts. 20:35

During the rise of industrial capitalism in the 19th and 20th centuries, we see the advent of the benevolent robber baron. John D. Rockefeller created his first foundation in 1913 as a direct response to the growing outcry against his accumulated wealth. Alexis De Tocqueville, observing the rumblings of philanthropy in America in the early-19th century, noted: "These groups did not see themselves as vehicles to promote virtue but rather as mechanisms through which the self-interest of individuals could be harnessed to work for the wider interests of society."[112]

This kind of economic functionalism, self-preservation, hubris and rationalism, as established by Carnegie and Rockefeller, emboldened the fourth and most recent incarnation of philanthropy into what is often referred to as institutional philanthropy, or, more recently, what has been described as "philanthrocapitalism".[113] Philanthrocapitalism focuses on market dynamics, specifically the individual's capacity to produce wealth within capitalism and to direct outcomes as its end function. Rather than the distribution of divine gifts, the central deity of this new approach is money itself, and the presumed intellectual and moral superiority that accompanies wealth accumulation.

There are two core myths of capitalism that have been reified and amplified since philanthropy's split from the Abrahamic notions of giving through the robber-baron model of industrial capitalism and now through the institutional philanthropic model under neoliberalism. The first is the myth that ordinary people do not know what is good for them and require the instruction of the wealthy class, whose wealth must be tied to superior skill or intelligence. The second is the ahistorical exoneration of wealth creation that produces the means for philanthropic enterprise in the first place.

We are conditioned to see the benevolence and wisdom attributed to those who have accumulated wealth. Becoming rich by any means necessary is perceived as the sole means by which one can then share abundance with the rest of the world.

---

[112] Vallely (2020), p.12

[113] The first articulation of this concept was written, in earnest, by the editor of *The Economist* Matthew Bishop and co-author Micheal Green in their 2008 ode to the white-saviour industrial complex, *Philanthrocapitalism: How the rich can save the world*. In this book, they actually say: "If the rich do not take on this responsibility, they risk provoking the public into a political backlash against the economic system that allowed them to become so wealthy...." See Bishop & Green (2010), p.30. For a considered counterpoint, see Shiva (Ed.) (2021).

The aim of philanthropy is to increase the capacity of others to have similar economic opportunities within the market system. Philanthropy has moved from a silencing salve for retribution against power elites to pro-active co-optation machinery, drawing in new converts into the church of market fundamentalism.

Philanthropy has forgotten the warning cry of Theodore Roosevelt: "No amount of charities in spending such fortunes can compensate in any way for the misconduct in acquiring them." To Roosevelt's point, we are suggesting that the historical understanding of whence the money came must be integrated into the manner in which we approach it. We will go deeper into the implications of this assertion in Part Three.

> *Philanthropy has moved from a silencing salve for retribution against power elites to pro-active co-optation machinery, drawing in new converts into the church of market fundamentalism.*

ARTWORK ON FOLLOWING PAGE:

"FREEDOM?"

~ VITTORIA CARDONA ~

REFLECTION EXERCISE:
INVOKING THE DEITY OF MONEY

...

- PAUSE -

...

For the purposes of this exercise, let us imagine money as a deity – a powerful god or supreme being that has its own agency, intentions, beliefs, characteristics and objectives.

Please write out your answers to the prompts below:

- What are the attributes, physical descriptors, and properties of the deity of money?
- What does it look like to you? Is it gendered? What colour is it? What does it smell like? If you could taste it, what would it taste like? How does it approach you when you invoke it?
- What are both the superpowers and shadows of money?
- What is your relationship like with this god? How does it treat you? How do you treat it?
- If you could say anything to this deity, what would you say? And why would you say this?
- What would this god say to you?
- When you think about money, where do you feel sensation in your body?
- Where do you believe your thoughts, feelings and desires about money come from?
- Have they changed throughout your life? Why and how?
- What other thought-forms are interrelated with money? Another way to ask this is, who would the god of money hang out with (e.g. scarcity, private property, elitism, desire, hunger, cannibalism, abundance, etc.)?
- What healing wants to happen through your evolving relationship with money?
- What does the deity of money want to become?

---

*Read through your reflections to these questions.
Notice how you feel as you go through your answers.*

THE THIRD HIERARCHY

~

INSTITUTIONS AS FRACTAL NODES UPHOLDING THE LOGIC OF PHILANTHROPY

> *"Ignorance*
> *Protects itself,*
> *And protected,*
> *Ignorance grows."*
> - Octavia E. Butler[114]

> *"And what do you benefit if you gain the*
> *whole world but lose your own soul?"*
> - Mark 8:36

A fractal is a geometric shape in which each part has the same characteristics as the whole, and similar patterns recur at progressively smaller scales. A node is simply a replicator or amplifier in a network.

Although individual foundations and philanthropists believe that they have agency, freedom, and can create self-contained strategies for addressing social issues, the notion of fractal nodes indicates the structural design of the economic system and the philanthropic sector, and how the concomitant constraints ensure the replication of the logic of the dominant culture.

As individuals, we are also incentivised to play out the dominant logic in our fractal realms, as we will see in the next section. Neoliberalism is a tightly-woven system that requires our collective complicity. Although we may know that every dollar of wealth created heats up the planet and creates more inequality, we are tied into the system through globalised supply chains, dependence on capital, a set of values, cultural norms, and other forces. We are lulled and/or coerced into a form of *distributed fascism* where we as individuals extract more, consume more, destroy

---
[114] Butler (2019)

more and accumulate more, in apparent competition with other 'rational actors', without ever being able to step back to see or act upon the totality of a more holistic worldview.[115] This logic of *distributed fascism* not only plays out in our acquisition and consumption, but also in philanthropy and our ways of giving, and receiving.

The institutions of philanthropy replicate the logic of neoliberalism through what we call the *four shadows of philanthropy* which include (but are not limited to) the following:

1. Privileging neoliberal notions of success so that making money equates to having the wisdom and requisite acumen for how to give money away.
2. Centering measurement and knowable impacts in order to control, justify, and quantify investments.
3. Viewing philanthropy as an entitlement and right of being wealthy.
4. Morally positioning philanthropy as inherently good, leading to perpetual growth of institutions and the sector as the ultimate goal.

Our aim here is not to critique individual foundations or wealth holders, but rather to examine and expose the deeper logics driving the culture of philanthropic institutions, which are also the same drivers of culture at large.

> *Although individual foundations and philanthropists believe that they have agency, freedom, and can create self-contained strategies for addressing social issues, the notion of fractal nodes indicates the structural design of the economic system and the philanthropic sector, and how the concomitant constraints ensure the replication of the logic of the dominant culture.*

---

[115] For a deeper explanation of distributed fascism, see Ladha (April 14, 2018).

1. SUCCESS:
MAKING MONEY EQUATES TO WISDOM IN GIVING MONEY

In some ways, the most glaring conceit of philanthropy is the belief that individuals who made their wealth in the marketplace of cutthroat capitalism must inherently be more intelligent, even to the point of omniscience; they can understand, dissect, strategise and solve the complex problems created by capitalism in the first place (Bill Gates, Jack Ma, Jeff Bezos and Chris Hohn are some examples that come to mind for many).

Let's unpack this for a moment. We have presented the neoliberal belief that the acquisition of wealth equates to life success and therefore justifies economic, moral and other forms of superiority. This belief then becomes institutionalised into a foundation or a set of giving practices that reinforce it through the hubris of attempting to solve and address deeply complex social problems created by the system these actors perpetuate and benefit from. This is then amplified by a Byzantine court of functionaries (those viewed as having the requisite expertise and professional experience) to carry out the "founder's vision" by pursuing a set of solutions and strategies that serve as the scaffolding for the court to operate within.

Setting up a foundation or family office for philanthropy has become another commodity in the marketplace of consumerist-status culture. Those who achieve a certain socio-economic strata often set up a foundation to show they have achieved the pinnacle of neoliberal success, wielding more power in political and social realms, receiving cultural kudos, and continuing to amass more wealth through tax breaks, transfer mispricing and other accounting and legal black magic.

As we have argued earlier, the dominant culture rewards those who best serve its logic of creating more capital. There is no correlation between wealth acquisition and cognitive or moral development. In fact, the research shows that the opposite is true; people who do well within the rigged game of industrial capitalism, and those who admire and emulate 'successful' capitalists, have higher correlations with amoral, sociopathic and even psychopathic behaviour.[116]

---

[116] Miller (June 29, 2012)

Moreover, both the initial donor(s) and the cadre of people recruited for philanthropic work are trained as bureaucrats and technocrats, disproportionately coming from 'elite' universities (usually public policy or business administration), and indoctrinated in the dominant business culture of acquisition, self-preservation, materialism, elitism, and positivism.

Most often, these functionaries do not have experience in care work, front-line service, community organising or other socially-motivated vocations that would help them be more proximate to or better understand the plight of the people most harmed by the existing system. They are usually from socio-economic classes that have been historically rewarded for their complicity with(in) capitalism. As a result of their social location, class, race, gender and assumed authority, they may not have developed the deep relational webs or inner resources that cultivate their capacity for empathy, nurture, care, generosity or solidarity.

This dearth of relevant experience and emotional capacity builds the edifice of the cultures at the heart of the institutions within philanthropy. As Tiokasin Ghosthorse, a Lakota elder, stated in an interview with the authors: "Philanthropy is made up of uninitiated people who feel entitled to solve the problems their culture created without understanding the impacts of their culture in the first place."[117]

II. MEASUREMENT:

CONTROLLING AND QUANTIFYING INVESTMENTS THROUGH METRICS

As neoliberalism continues to produce more individual philanthropies, we see a replication of the dominant culture when it comes to measuring 'success'. Many foundations have borrowed from business culture the idea of *key performance indicators* or metrics of success. These are often arbitrary statistics subjectively attuned to each 'problem to be solved', showing the progress that has been made with the 'funder's money' to ensure efficiency and success.

Most foundations develop strategic plans, reviewed periodically, based on their analysis of what issues are most pressing and what types of grants and activities

---

[117] Ghosthorse (June 12, 2021)

(beyond the grant dollars) would lead to the most 'impact'. There is often an implicit belief that a foundation's institutional culture can learn and benefit from the way the market behaves and solves problems (this is often labelled as 'professionalisation').

Others herald *strategic philanthropy* or *outcomes-based philanthropy* as the best use of the grant dollars to advance narrowly defined impact measures.[118] There is also a growing field of practice around *effective altruism*, an arbitrary but seductive school of thought that believes one can rationally decide where the most philanthropic impact can happen based on emotive metrics like 'saving lives' without examining the broader structural drivers or the funder's internal psychological landscape.[119]

Some funders celebrate the success of individual actors to such an extent that they set up awards and celebrate the 'social entrepreneur' or other hero archetypes as winners of the game to best solve complex problems (which of course, inherently reinforces competition and ignores the collaborative and collective nature of both the problems and vectors of change). Most institutions believe it is their core objective and indeed responsibility to dissect, deduce, and then determine what is best for the world and which individuals are the most apt 'leaders' to fulfil their mandated missions.

Just as many who acquire wealth believe it is solely due to their own hard work, ingenuity, superiority of skill & talent and other individual attributes, potential grantees must also demonstrate their deservedness under similar criteria when applying for grants. This occurs through well-formed "theories-of-change" (essentially the business case or linear-chain argument to validate an organisation, project, or movement's strategy in the eyes of the funder); through the ability to complete rigorous grant application processes and impending milestone reports (written by and for particular intelligence types, biassing for class, education, race, gender, access, etc.); and through their ability and acumen at maintaining relationships with program officers and other decision-makers within a foundation.

---

[118] *Outcomes-based philanthropy* was an internal school of thought that came to prominence in the early 2000s that based philanthropic giving on ideal strategic outcomes that were desired rather than other factors such as relationships, trust or emerging contexts.

[119] *Effective altruism* is a term that was coined by the Australian moral philosopher Peter Singer in the early 2000s and has since spawned a global following, largely amongst white males. For a deeper look at the failure of effective altruism to address systemic causes see Clough (2015).

The implications of these practices and cultures are dire: they create a sub-stratum of grantees who report to *de facto* managers (i.e. the program officer); they uphold the belief in technical, rationally-defined problems without a historical or structural analysis; they reify the individual rational actor as someone who can personally determine what is good for society; they reinforce the linearity of cause-and-effect logic and commodify social/care work (i.e. if you fund x, you will get y results); they perpetuate the belief that more information will save us; they reinforce the materialist, Newtonian logic that problems are individual puzzle pieces in a machine that can be understood and solved (further reinforcing the world-as-machine metaphor); and, critically, all of these practices do not address the underlying causes of the problems in the first place (i.e. a growth-based economic system built on historical injustices).

As a result, most foundations ignore the intersectionality of life, identity, and social issues. Philanthropy belies the complexity of political and ecological problems, continuing to fund the same instruments for social change even when they do not work and the meta-crisis deepens.

III. ENTITLEMENT:
GIVING IS A RIGHT OF DESERVED WEALTH

One might ask why foundations behave in these ways, and replicate cultures that perpetuate the problems they ostensibly want to address. Given the structural-systems approach to culture we have invoked throughout this book, one can see that there is one critical imported bias from the neoliberal operating system; namely, that *giving is an extension of acquiring.*

Since the initial money was 'created' within the God-like stratum of the market, it was fairly, justly and deservedly earned and, therefore, it is the individual's choice to do what they will with those funds, in whatever way, and wherever they desire. That is freedom; the freedom of choice that comes from being a winner in the market system. This freedom also includes removing funding from grantee partners at whim, often without dialogue or accountability (this is one of the major grievances we heard from foundation partners).

There is a formula at the motivational core here: *Good intentions plus capital equals the right to enter the social sphere to 'solve problems' for other beings.* With this right-to-give comes other entitlements, including the right-to-know that the funds are being deployed in a way that is satisfactory to those providing the grants.

With this right-to-know externally also comes a right-to-privacy internally. Wealth holders can set up a tax shelter as a formal organisation or through a donor-advised fund (see previous section for more context) that can then intervene and influence society, according to the desires and ways of seeing and being that the wealthy enact, with anonymity.

Each institution can decide to exist for whatever length of time it sees fit and invest dollars in capital markets to continue the institution indefinitely. The donors can decide on the type of institution they will run, who is on the board, as well as benefiting from the power society confers to say that this is a worthy endeavour and use of tax dollars. Again, this stems from the worldview and practice of philanthropy as an extension of the free market and colonialism.

Like colonial powers of the past, philanthropy often does not consider if it is welcomed in a given country, context, or community that it wants to operate in and make grants to. Instead, the dominant assumption is that because more money is better, and money creates social change, the philanthropic institution can decide where to work, what issues matter, who is worthy of support, how change happens in a given context, and what knowledge shall be preserved.

We are accustomed to thinking about extraction of minerals and natural resources; philanthropy often traffics in the extraction of information, funding research surveys in the poorest communities without asking or deeply listening to what those communities' priorities are or considering how they may benefit.

Since philanthropy is an extension of the hegemony of the geopolitical North, it is often situated within the ideals of the "white saviour industrial complex"[120]. Simply put, it is the *white gaze* on poverty and disease that permeates most of philanthropy. The deeper motivations, narratives, and behaviours that accompany this gaze go largely unquestioned and too often unseen.

---

[120] Cole (March 21, 2012)

This is probably why there is very little discourse or concern about accountability or scrutiny of foundations. These are the choices of the individuals whose money it is, whose manifest destiny is saving the poor, and their courts of administrators who are paid to make the saviour's dreams a reality.

IV. GROWTH:
PHILANTHROPY IS MORALLY GOOD, THEREFORE THE GROWTH OF PHILANTHROPY IS EVEN BETTER

We will now end this section with the most nefarious shadow at the heart of philanthropy – growth itself.

The very existence of most foundations is based on the core assumption of growth. Growth as a means for perpetuity. Growth as a proxy for expanding power and success in the marketplace of solutions. Growth as expansion of the imperium of goodness and benevolence that is philanthropy.

There are many rationalisations for the "growth is good" worldview, the most prominent being that philanthropy has an obligation to grow its endowment capital for 'future beneficiaries'.[121] Since larger endowments mean more grants, this equates to more 'good' in the world. As the current president of the Ford Foundation states, "endowment is the engine of the work, and the capital markets keep that engine fueled and firing."[122] Foundations are ranked according to their endowment size and a core premise of institutional philanthropy is that those with bigger endowments wield more influence and power.

The negative consequences of growing endowments through the life-destruction machine of capital markets, despite recent calls for divestment in fossil fuels, is almost never questioned. Hence, we have a record number of foundations in existence, many of which have been set up in the last twenty years, with enormous and fast-growing endowments propping up the current economic system they believe they are addressing the symptoms of.

---

[121] Kramer (January 4, 2021)
[122] Walker (January 4, 2021)

> *The very existence of most foundations is based on the core assumption of growth. Growth as a means for perpetuity. Growth as a proxy for expanding power and success in the marketplace of solutions. Growth as expansion of the imperium of goodness and benevolence that is philanthropy.*

As the influence, prestige and power of these institutions grows, the democratic process of deciding who gets access to these funds is thwarted by a small philanthropic plutocracy making unaccountable decisions by whim to those who have proximity to philanthropic power and can get access to foundations and complete the language and cognitive puzzles of laborious application forms designed for and by philanthropic elites.

Moreover, the assumption that the work these philanthropic institutions are doing is inherently good is almost never questioned. The idea of 'effective philanthropy' masks what is being measured, what can even be measured, and what the biases of those doing the measurement are because the belief in the inherent goodness of philanthropy is at the very root of each institution's blindness.

One interviewee, the long-time philanthropic elder Barry Knight, summarised what he calls the sins of philanthropic institutions as "Ego, Silo, Halo, and Logo".[123] It starts with the inflated ego that believes an individual or foundation can address deep, complex societal problems with little to no prior relevant experience or relationships in a given field. That doing so requires dissecting these problems into arbitrary or siloed categories that are subjectively chosen (what they may call strategy). That these acts of benevolence require societal acknowledgement (from tax breaks to banquets to a social aura of goodness). And finally, the requisite attribution must be given to the funder, not the practitioner implementing this work, as society's work could not be achieved without the magnanimity of philanthropy.

In summary, there are a series of unquestioned assumptions when setting up and operating a foundation: a corporation, wealthy person or family has the right to

---

[123] Knight (September 28, 2021)

set up and operate as a foundation (for whatever length of time they decide); they have the intelligence to identify the most pressing social and ecological problems; they have the know-how to solve them and robust-enough relationships and access to practitioners who know how to execute their preconceived solutions; they have the right to decide who is worthy (or not) of resources and support; and they have the legitimacy to operate in perpetuity with little public accountability or scrutiny. This is by no means an exhaustive list. Our aim is to highlight the deeper logics and unexamined narratives that shape and constrain foundations and their activities.

In short, it is never questioned that the logic that created the meta-crisis may not be the appropriate logic to address its consequences. It is never made explicit that perpetuating the existence of foundations may be doing more harm than good. It is never asked if the dying of the old may be necessary to midwife the birth of the new.

> *The idea of 'effective philanthropy' masks what is being measured, what can even be measured, and what the biases of those doing the measurement are because the belief in the inherent goodness of philanthropy is at the very root of each institution's blindness.*

REFLECTION EXERCISE: ENTITLEMENT VERSUS ENTRUSTMENT

- PAUSE -

...

Reflect on the Sufi proverb on the opposite page
and then answer the questions below:

...

- How is entitlement connected to thought-forms of deserving, ownership, and rights? How do you conceive or would you define entrustment?
- What do you feel entitled to, materially, emotionally and spiritually? Why do you feel entitled to these things?
- What have you been entrusted with? Why do you think you were entrusted with these endowments and gifts?
- How would a shift from the logic of "rights and entitlements" to one of "entrustment and entanglements" affect both your personal life and as a practitioner within the philanthropic sector?
- Do you believe you are entitled to continue your philanthropic and/or social change work? If so, why? If not, why not?

"

You are entrusted with everything
and entitled to nothing.

"

- *Sufi proverb*

THE FOURTH HIERARCHY

~

INDIVIDUALS AS REPLICATORS OF NEOLIBERAL LOGIC

"The true system, the real system, is our present construction of systematic thought itself, rationality itself, and if a factory is torn down but the rationality which produced it is left standing, then that rationality will simply produce another factory. If a revolution destroys a systematic government, but the systematic patterns of thought that produced that government are left intact, then those patterns will repeat themselves in the succeeding government. There's so much talk about the system. And so little understanding."

- Robert M. Pirsig[124]

"Did you know that there are some people that are so poor that all they have is money?"

- Bob Marley

We have started to sketch out a shared understanding of the logic of our current system, neoliberal capitalism. We have described how the philanthropic sector is both an extension and externalisation of this system. And we have described how individual institutions are fractal nodes replicating the dominant logic. Now we will turn our gaze to the individuals at the heart of these institutions.

Of course, it is impossible to talk about people within philanthropy with any sense of uniformity. There is such a broad range of practitioners, from program officers working in foundations, activist funders attempting to disrupt the sector, board members, wealth holders, and the plethora of advisors on the periphery from financial advisors, management consultants, accountants, lawyers, consiglieres, family members, coaches, therapists and even personal gurus. And of course, grantees,

---
[124] Pirsig (1974), p.94

their professionalised paid staff, as well as the intended 'recipients' of philanthropy's beneficence, are also deeply implicated in the cultural and relational fabric that weaves the sector into becoming.

For the sake of simplicity, we will break out two broad groups of people. Those whose financial resources are being deployed, whom we will call *wealth holders* and those who give away these resources, whom we will call *wealth granters*. Of course, there are wealth holders who directly give grants themselves, and for that overlapping Venn, we will ask the reader to discern when one or both of the descriptors are relevant.

As we researched a vast swath of literature about philanthropy, money, gifting, activism, systemic change, reparations and other relevant topics, as well as through our interviews with practitioners, we were surprised by the dearth of psycho-spiritual insights as to what motivates people to engage with philanthropy. Before we go deeper into the motivational landscape of wealth holders and wealth granters, we will first start with an insight about the individuals across the spectrum of philanthropy.

What was clear from the hundred plus interviews we conducted was two main insights. The first is that the vast majority of people believe the current model of philanthropy is not working, yet they believe they cannot break out of the existing paradigm. We will call this the *philanthropic paradox of powerlessness*. The second is that there was an almost universal motivational interest in wielding power (which also includes control, status, entitlement as well as the well-meaning intent of contributing to change) yet a dearth of understanding of the consequences or responsibilities this power may have. We will call this the *philanthropic paradox of power*.

The juxtaposition of the *paradox of powerlessness* and the *paradox of power* leads to a striking image of a seemingly helpless elite class of philanthropic decision-makers who sense the dominant paradigm coming to an end; a recognition that their existing seat is a privileged, albeit temporary position; and a careless, almost callous disposition towards what more or what else could be done given their circumstance, access to wealth, and existing power base.

Of course, on one level, this may feel like a caricature of the sector, when in fact there are countless others who do not feel powerless and are trying to grapple with their power and privilege in earnest. On another level, this description could also be true of any ordinary beneficiary or bureaucrat of the capitalist system who has a sense of the impending cascade of crises but carries on as they are.

However, what is unique about philanthropy is the disproportionate power it has as a sector, largely determining the activities and parameters of civil society, actively reinforcing the status quo, all the while receiving the benefits of directing public funds, including tax breaks and social legitimacy. Also, given how interwoven philanthropy is with the fabric of society – community organisers, activists, cultural centres, educational institutions, care workers, etc. – it is critical to examine the dynamics and drivers of individuals within the sector.

> *The juxtaposition of the paradox of powerlessness and the paradox of power leads to a striking image of a seemingly helpless elite class of philanthropic decision-makers who sense the dominant paradigm coming to an end; a recognition that their existing seat is a privileged, albeit temporary, position; and a careless, almost callous disposition towards what more or what else could be done given their circumstance, access to wealth, and existing power base.*

Through our interviews with grantees and practitioners, three dominant ideas or thought-forms continuously appeared in the dialogue and discourse: (1) Control (2) Victimhood and (3) Entitlement. Grantees often felt controlled, cajoled and manipulated into performing certain types of work that must be delivered and presented in foundation-friendly formats. When describing the broader economic system or cultural context, the language of victimisation and victimhood was strong and persistent. Many activists and organisers felt forced into the work they do as a result of what is happening in the external world, and sometimes from the mandate of a foundation's interests. One of the most consistent critiques of philanthropy was its sense of entitlement through various guises (e.g. assumed knowledge or superiority, lack of participatory processes, enforced cultural norms, and other "power-over" approaches).

What we serendipitously came to realise is that these three thought-forms of control, victimhood and entitlement map quite neatly to the Karpman Drama Triangle.[125] In 1968, the psychologist Stephen Karpman developed the Drama Triangle as part of his research in the Transactional Analysis school of psychotherapy to better understand the dynamics of conflict. His three archetypal roles were the rescuer, persecutor and victim.

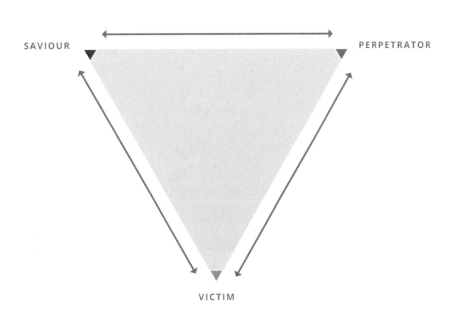

For the sake of our present discourse on philanthropy, we will rename the "rescuer" archetype as the "saviour" so as to better describe the role vis-a-vis grant-making. Essentially, the saviour's motivation is to 'solve' problems as a means of controlling the external environment, to control peoples and events, and to be seen as a necessary good within the social context. Of course, philanthropy has the external complexities of benefiting financially, reputationally and in terms of proximity to power. The net effect is that philanthropy creates a *dependency effect*, further exacerbating the victim archetype and never truly confronting its own inner contradictions, biases, or benefits. Nor is the broader operating system of neoliberalism ever challenged as a structural-historical analysis is rarely a consideration for funders in the first place. As we will discuss later, *privilege is a constraint* and most people who benefit

---

[125] Karpman (2014)

from existing systems cannot hold a constellational or systems-based worldview that allows them to sufficiently understand the context from whence these social issues arise in the first place.

This is not to say that philanthropy solely plays the 'saviour' archetypal role. Within the complexity of social dynamics, all actors play the roles of all three archetypes, as these feeling states rotate in time, context, and social location. For example, the activist grantee may go on to play the saviour role in their local community, or as the well-funded NGO which has disproportionate influence in a particular issue area.

The role of persecutor or perpetrator is often played by a corporation, government, institution, law, policy (and so on) that the activist or not-for-profit is raising money to address and confront. The irony of course is that the perpetrator is often the domain of wealth-creation that gives rise to the systemic injustices in the first place, including wealth concentration, and subsequently, philanthropy.

The perpetrators are often driven by a sense of deep entitlement. They believe they have the right to extract resources from other peoples' lands, to enact policies that affect others without consultation or reciprocity, or to enslave populations as and when it serves their agenda. Nevertheless, as we externalise blame, the two sides of funders and grantees triangulate their problems in a shared front, never confronting their own inner landscapes (e.g. how they are in conflict by their investment or consumption decisions) or the broader social context (i.e. the debt-based, growth-dependent system) that perpetuates the drama cycle in the first place.

Moreover, the perpetrator can often feel like the victim as well. We have often heard employees of large foundations, or even neoliberal organisations like the World Bank, commiserating over the fact that the people who are resisting their 'development' projects do not understand how the contested projects are in "their best interests".

This plays out in the way individuals in foundations operate, especially in cross-cultural contexts. The program officer who works on X issue, will only fund those who do Y in the ways they see as effective, within the purview of their foundation's strategy, grant-making, results requirements and areas of interest. To those receiving grants, this can seem like a "power-over" paradigm where the foundation is determining the agenda based on how they see the problem and solution; deciding who, what, and where are the most deserving ways to pursue change; and determining what is worthy (or 'impactful', 'innovative', 'strategic', or any other such term). If these logics are questioned, or if the power dynamics are pointed out, it very quickly can turn into a defensive or dismissive posture as their superiority is questioned.

Society reinforces the perpetrator as hero through the cultural obsession with expertise, winning, garnering followers, and other more seemingly benign expressions of domination. For philanthropy, this plays out in the public celebration of philanthropy's social contribution (e.g. from media attention to award galas to tax breaks).

DRAMA TRIANGLE WITH DOMINANT THOUGHT-FORMS

SAVIOUR/CONTROL

PERPETRATOR/ENTITLEMENT

VICTIM/VICTIMHOOD

Finally, the role of victim is often enacted by affected communities, activists and organisers who are raising funds to address critical social issues. Their dependency on philanthropy makes them beholden – both through their immediate plight and via their means of livelihood – to a powerful beneficiary who arbitrarily chooses by whim what, how and when they can work on issues that are often existential to their lives and their communities. Importantly, the perceived victims often become perpetrators, advancing identity politics, binary logic (e.g. us-versus-them), and othering behaviours.

The victimhood thought-form also shows itself more subtly in an attachment to scarcity and comfort. The scarcity mindset shows up quite frequently, even in endowed institutions, as programs lament the lack of sufficient grant dollars to pursue desired changes, or the lack of 'worthy' organisations to support. The victim archetype can also show up when individuals feel overpowered by the board, by leadership, by the strategy, by the need to uphold expertise and be professional, by the sheer amount of work, and other drivers.

At a fundamental level, including the somatic, most people in philanthropy have a sense of the radical, discontinuous change that is being manifested through catastrophic climate change, ecological collapse, perpetual war, egregious inequality, inhumane poverty and disproportionate access to resources, yet most people cannot break out of the Saviour-Perpetrator-Victim/Control-Entitlement-Victimhood cycle. Consciously or unconsciously, they are caught up in the momentum of the current paradigm; it may, if faced, even seem life-threatening to step out of it.[126]

As the Nigerian poet and philosopher Bayo Akomolafe reminded us: "Part of the crisis is the way we are responding to the crisis."[127] Within the halls of philanthropy, internal contradictions, let alone active contributions to the crisis, are rarely interrogated and we rarely hear conversations about how what is going on in the 'outside world' affects each of us directly and internally. Nor how the continuation of the neoliberal logic of hierarchy, private property, wealth hoarding, separation, control, entitlement and victimhood can be found at the very root of the problems we are trying to solve through institutions born and perpetuated through and with the dominant logic.

---

[126] Buie (12 July 2021)
[127] Akomolafe (March 11, 2020)

REFLECTION EXERCISE:
SEEING THROUGH THE DRAMA TRIANGLE

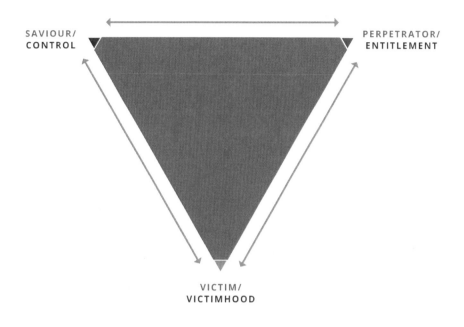

- PAUSE -

Stand up and embody the posture of each archetype, one at a time.
First the saviour, then perpetrator, and then victim.

...

Please write out your answers to the prompts below:

- What shapes/forms did you make with your body? Were you sitting, standing or lying down? What were you doing with your hands, legs, facial expressions and heart?
- Where were you looking?
- What associations (images, words, sensations, vibrations, feelings) came up with each posture?
- What did it feel like to go from the saviour to the perpetrator? And then the perpetrator to the victim?

- PAUSE -

Now shake your body and relax. Take a neutral posture.
Breathe deeply for a few breaths.

...

Then go back to your journal to answer the following:

- Where and how do you see the three archetypal roles playing out in the philanthropic sector? How do they play out in your organisation? How do they play out in your personal life?
- When and how have you been the saviour, perpetrator and victim and when do you move between them? Which one(s) are harder or easier for you to identify with?
- Which one is your 'home base' (e.g. dominant archetype)? Why do you think that is?
- When and how do you engage with the thought-forms of Control, Entitlement and Victimhood? How do they play out in your body? What activates or precipitates these states or behaviours in you, your loved ones, your colleagues, your experience of the world around you? Where do you think you learned these behaviours?
- What methods could or do you use to move out of the Drama Triangle?
- What would it look like in philanthropy to step out of the triangle? What would have to change? What is in the way of that change? What is currently supportive of such changes?

SUPERIORITY OF WEALTH HOLDERS

There is another important factor that blinds the beneficiaries of the system from seeing its true nature: *the current order validates their position in the moral hierarchy.* If the world is getting better, it is largely because of wealth creators – rational, educated, liberal-minded, white. Those who exemplify these attributes deserve the exploits of playing the game well.[128] Especially if they believe they are "raising all boats" to bring the rest of us with them.[129] This is then amplified by our culture, especially through the neoliberal organ of the mass media, lionising the achievements of these individuals and idealising their lives and attributes.

We do not highlight these issues to denigrate wealth holders, but, rather, to point towards the social conditions and cultural context that we are all entangled with. These are the conditions from which philanthropy is created and perpetuated. In better understanding this context, we have a stronger probability of breaking the drama cycle.

SURVIVAL INSTINCT OF WEALTH GRANTERS

Many of the people we interviewed for this project are well meaning, good-intentioned people who have chosen a career path they believe will benefit others. Of course, they are embedded within a system that requires them to serve a financial power in order to survive, to pay bills, to put food on the table. In some ways, they are better informed (and can accept the deeper truths of our times more readily than wealth-holders) about the interwoven meta-crisis and the looming discontinuous change that is on the horizon, and already here for the majority of the world.

One interviewee described those who work in philanthropy as living in "the first-class sleeping quarters of the Titanic." Adding, "most people within philanthropy are trying to be as comfortable as possible for as long as possible."[130] Another interviewee said "most people in philanthropy are trying to survive capitalism, in

---

[128] Here we are not referring to "whiteness" as simply a physical attribute but a psycho-social construct imbued with a corresponding worldview. See Menakem (2017) for a deeper dive into whiteness as a cultural construct.

[129] Ladha & Kirk (February 24, 2020)

[130] Anonymous (September 21, 2021)

whatever ways that means to them."[131] Of course, this is true for most human beings alive at this moment. However, the distinction is that most people in philanthropy have disproportionately high levels of privilege, and are paid to focus on solving social problems and understanding the contextual implications of the meta-crisis.

Through our research, we have subjectively deduced three primary archetypes amongst wealth granters: *apparatchiks, alchemists, and assassins*. Of course, as with all archetypes, any person can simultaneously enact one or more of these roles at a time, and can also move between roles. What is critical about archetypes is that through repetition, they partly determine what we believe to be real. In *Cosmos and History: The Myth of the Eternal Return*, the religious scholar Mircea Eliade defines the historical role of archetypes as such: "An object or an act becomes real only insofar as it imitates or repeats an archetype. Thus, reality is acquired solely through repetition or participation; everything which lacks an exemplary model is 'meaningless', i.e. it lacks reality."[132]

We will start with the most dominant archetype in philanthropy: the *apparatchik*. The term apparatchik has been used disparagingly since it was first employed to describe functionaries of the Communist Party of the USSR. Essentially, they are paid technocrats who enact orders in a chain-of-command, despite the nature of the orders or the consequences. For our purposes, we are referring to practitioners who rarely question given operating procedures within their institutions or organisations. They may feel autonomy in developing strategies, choosing grantees, monitoring progress, yet, as we've discussed above, this too is bound within the logic of neoliberalism (including colonialism, white supremacy, patriarchy, etc.). Their primary, underlying motivation is largely self-survival and job protection. A large proportion of people working in philanthropy are primarily situated in this first category, most of the time.

The second archetype, the *alchemist*, offered us some inspiration in our research. These people play a "bridge" role, often seeing themselves as allies of grantees, partners and activists. They often enact a healing function, shifting the relational and power dynamics to be more humane. Alchemists are experts in understanding and enacting "state-change". They transmute money, energy, conversations, and

---

[131] Anonymous (July 22, 2021)
[132] Eliade (1954), p.34

relational lines into the source material for life-centric models. They often function with high intuition and emotional intelligence, and do their work without creating strong conflict or tension among the wealth holders and/or boards of directors as they are masters of translation across worldviews and contexts.

The final archetype of the *assassin* plays a far more disruptive role. Although they may have similar educational and class backgrounds to others in their organisation, like the alchemist they may have shifted their motivational landscape into a deeper place of reciprocity, solidarity, generosity and altruism. They often see their role as organisers and movement builders and are willing to disrupt and risk their own livelihoods to enact social change. One of their dominant characteristics is that they are not seeking external validation, and often prefer helping things happen behind the scenes without acknowledgement of approval.

Some of the interviewees that we could categorise in this archetype made it explicit that their goals include addressing the heart of dominant practices, behaviours, memes, and cultural mores within the organisation including dispelling the belief that philanthropy is doing something important for grantees, addressing notions of entitlement and making visible neoliberal ideologies, behavioural practices and the very manner in which the organisation perceives and approaches grant-making. Many of them also stated that they would only play a role within philanthropy for a limited period of time, which would help increase their ability to take risks.

By stating the three archetypes we encountered, our aim here is not to disparage the apparatchik, as we realise that any particular actor can and does play various archetypal roles within certain contexts. We are not exempt from this and have also historically played all three of these roles in certain contexts.

We also want to reiterate that we are not trying to scapegoat 'bad actors'. We live within the complex, adaptive, evolutionary system of late-stage capitalism. In *Voltaire's Bastards*, the philosopher John Ralston Saul argues that we assume that people of merit rise to the top of the system. But in fact, the system finds the people that are best constructed to further its own existence, and draws them to the top.[133] In other words, those who most strongly believe and embody the values and behaviours of neoliberalism will be rewarded with what the system has to offer.

---

[133] Saul (2013)

REFLECTION EXERCISE:
NESTED HIERARCHIES OF THE DOMINANT PHILANTHROPIC SECTOR

Number of People Affected

We've described one articulation of the dominant philanthropic sector and the nested hierarchies flowing from the neoliberal operating system.

• • •

For this exercise, we would like you to draw your own nested hierarchy according to the following questions:

- How would you structure and describe the nested hierarchies of the global economic operating system and dominant philanthropy's role within it? What shape would it take? As you structure this, notice where you agree or disagree with how philanthropy and the social change sector (e.g. NGOs and civil society) are fractal nodes upholding the logic of neoliberalism.

- Do you agree with the three primary archetypes within philanthropy – *apparatchiks, alchemists and assassins*? If not, what other archetypes would you include? Which, if any, do you identify with? Which do you aspire to? How do these archetypal roles contribute to creating the nested hierarchy of neoliberal pyramid logic?

- Where did you feel agency, stagnation, dread, inspiration, resistance when reading the sections above? Can you track where these feelings live in your body and how they are expressed?

- What inner thought-forms and motivations keep you in your current role (e.g. safety, security, status, power, influence, certainty, experience, fear, the desire to help, solidarity, etc.)?

We have all created our own stories in order to feel comfortable and safe within a dying system. Many people believe they're helping the poor, mitigating climate change, and improving lives, and in limited ways, this may be true. But by accepting and then validating the logic at the heart of the system, we are in fact ensuring that the murky waters of the status quo stay toxic, continuing to pursue incrementalist reforms. Moreover, we are not, on the whole, looking deeper to see the birthplace and inherent blindspots of these dominant logics.

So far, we have situated philanthropy in the neoliberal operating system and described how it is born of, upholds, and exacerbates the machinery of capitalism. We touched on how philanthropy reinforces the dominant culture (including extraction, colonisation, imperialism, white supremacy, patriarchy, violence, and trauma).

Philanthropy is at a crossroads. We can continue to benefit from capital expansion based on an extractive, growth-dependent system that requires perpetual war and the exploitation of living systems, human and more-than-human, or we can use existing capital to usher in a transition to *life-centric economic models* in the short window of time that capital is still useful. Philanthropy can remain a by-product of industrial and technological capitalism or it can become a critical catalyst to support post capitalist realities.

PART TWO

FROM PARADOX TO EMERGING POSSIBILITIES

FROM PARADOX TO EMERGING POSSIBILITIES
~

"Time is not an arrow relentlessly moving forward, but something circular and strange, more akin to a lake in which the past, present and future exist."
- Robin Wall Kimmerer[14]

"Abundance is not the manifestation of physical wealth. It is the absence of scarcity of the heart."
- Pir Aga Mir

Through our research and many conversations with philanthropists, movement leaders, Indigenous elders, economists, anthropologists, grassroots organisers and others, there emerged a shared sense of possibility in the midst of the neoliberal desert. There was also a collective acknowledgement of the bifurcations of our times: the regressive threats of fascist authoritarianism, fear-based xenophobia, structural racism, primitive accumulation, rampant consumption, techno-utopianisism, amongst all the other drivers/consequences of neoliberalism. But all this came along too with a simultaneous blossoming and strengthening of lived possibilities for post capitalist alternatives.

Although this bifurcation is by no means well-balanced, these adjacent realities are rising through the cracks of the crumbling edifice of late-stage capitalism. We met dozens of practitioners who were aligning to become part of a growing response to the dominant vision of philanthropy, recognising the deep contradictions within the sector, critiquing its ongoing capitalist-colonialist practices, and sounding out the potential for radical change. This group is now burgeoning into a trans-local movement with the aim of galvanising a growing response to our current crisis through the unifying calls for just, equitable, responsible, sober and courageous responses to the meta-crisis. In what follows, we summarise some of the emerging lines of action and transition strategies.

---

[14] Quoted in Taylor (2019)

CALLS FOR JUST TRANSITION

~

Although there are many different frames, ideologies and communities that unite progressive funders and movements, for the purposes of convenience and coherence, we will use the familiar term of the *Just Transition (JT)* movement.[135] As with post capitalism, JT's starting premise is that we are at a crucial crossroads as a species; collapse processes are already underway and these are unevenly distributed to the detriment of the majority of humanity who live in the geopolitical global South.

In order to avoid a worst-case scenario and liberate ourselves from life-destroying structures, we must transition out of exploitative and extractive systems into regenerative, inclusive economies that address historical harms while creating equitable, just outcomes. In philanthropy, this often manifests as support for projects in the following areas: climate mitigation and adaptation; reforming existing governance structures; economic inclusion; and ensuring food, energy, water and cultural sovereignty, amongst other initiatives.

In order to better understand the JT movement, we will look at specific initiatives through the lens of the *Three Horizons framework*, postulated by Bill Sharpe.[136] Sharpe's simple, pragmatic framework is currently used across many sectors to temporally conceptualise (i.e. map efforts over successive periods of time) what is needed to disrupt current systems and to transition into new patterns. In his book *Three Horizons: The Patterning of Hope* he says: "The essence of *Three Horizons* practice is to develop both an individual and a shared awareness of all three horizons, seeing them as perspectives that must all come into the discussion, and to work flexibly with the contributions that each one makes to the continuing process of renewal on which we all depend. We step out of our individual mindset into a shared space of creative possibility."[137]

Horizon 1 is characterised by sustaining *business as usual*, often focusing on reform efforts that do not fundamentally challenge the deeper logics of current systems.

---

[135] For more about history, demands and articulations of the JT movement, see Climate Justice Alliance (2018).
[136] Sharpe (2020)
[137] Sharpe (2020), p.26

For example, within philanthropy, this includes efforts to improve democracy, advance green economy initiatives, reform education, etc. Horizon 2 represents *disruptive innovation*, which creates transition pathways that transform or render Horizon 1 efforts irrelevant to varying degrees. At the point where Horizon 2 innovations become more effective than the existing practices, they begin to replace aspects of Horizon 1. Some forms of disruptive innovation ultimately get co-opted and absorbed by Horizon 1, while other forms of innovation can serve as bridge pathways from Horizon 1 to Horizon 3.

Horizon 3 is how we envision the *unknowable, emergent future*. We may not be able to define this future in detail, but we can articulate principles and practices as preconditions and pathways. The term *horizons* also suggests that we can see towards, but not over, a common vista. Thus, as we look towards Horizon 2, we conjure Horizon 3 as the *coordinates of possibility*.

When we map the various efforts currently underway, we see the JT movement as primarily inhabiting Horizon 1 (e.g. stopping fossil fuel extraction, labour-union organising to promote better livelihoods, etc.) with some expanding efforts in Horizon 2 (e.g. direct democracy & governance, localised production and consumption, decolonising philanthropy itself, etc.). The JT movement within philanthropy is heavily focused on funding advocacy to reform and dismantle systems of oppression, including current institutions, cultures, economies, and polities.

While the actual dismantling of these structures and the creation of alternative systems is the work of Horizon 2, the advocacy itself remains by and large a Horizon 1 activity. That is, the deeper logics of the current dominant culture, including continuing the growth-debt model, remain unaddressed in much of the advocacy efforts. For example, one of the JT movement's demands is the need to redistribute capital and power more evenly; however, this does not halt exploitative production of capital in the first place, and nor does it include a nuanced consideration of how the related thought-forms of greed, exploitation, commodification and scarcity run in and through us, feeding and reinforcing the broader neoliberal operating system and its related systems of domination and exploitation.

Of course, redistribution of capital and power is a necessary, short-term, Horizon 1 re-balancing transition pathway. However, by pursuing it, there is a risk that redistribution may become an endgame in and of itself (i.e. more equity for surviving capitalism and upholding modernity). The work to dismantle and establish pre-conditions for Horizon 2 gets conflated and contorted into such ends, calcifying the temporal focus into improving conditions for a slightly better existence within Horizon 1.[138]

Also, the JT movement often upholds an assumption of the linearity of time and a directionality of progress; in other words, we are moving from A to B, from old to new, and this direction *inherently* represents progress. This sequential form belies the messy, haptic, nonlinear, simultaneous nature of social change and the parallel realities that are already being created and lived simultaneously.

Embedded in this assumption of linearity is a binary logic. Where, in the old system, power was (and is) consolidated amongst elites, governments & corporations, in the emerging system power will be consolidated in and through communities and movements. Although this will be a necessary part of a larger process, transferring power from one group to another is not necessarily a definitive solution. Such redistribution does not emancipate us from the thought-forms that underlie our tendency to abuse power or dominate, as countless revolutions and social movements have shown us over the past few hundred years.

Within some manifestations of the JT framing, there is a focus on our existing polity (i.e. nation-states and the rule of law) and often a view that change happens by persuading elites to give up power. In so doing, these articulations of the JT still legitimate and reify the existing institutions of traditional power structures. We do not believe that this was the original intention of the JT movement. Of course, a focus on the existing structures of power may be necessary for changes within Horizon 1, but these old structures cannot remain as the ceilings of our political imagination.

Moreover, the current articulation of JT may not allow for what some activists and thinkers refer to as the third way – a non-dualistic creolisation, or the creation of

---

[138] For a useful analysis of the pernicious deeper logics that drive not only philanthropy but the entire NGO industrial complex (and mainstream civil society), see Smith (2007).

"fugitive epistemologies" to use the language of Bayo Akomolafe, where the old and emergent begin to remix and create something yet unknown. In an interview with the authors, Bayo invited us into the potential for 'disorientation': the loss of the coordinates that tell us who we are, who the so-called other is, and how the world must be. He suggested that philanthropy should study the cracks or borderlands, the marginal spaces where possibility can open; the chasm between the seemingly fixed world we believe we know and the not-yet worlds to come.

Bayo uses the language of postactivism to articulate what may emerge from this non-binary approach. He says, "Postactivism is the material manifestation of all the linkages that we are imbricated with; those that call into question our claims to linear exertion of agency. The activist is no longer the same. In a post-anthropocentric world, the activist is now a web. So the activist is, in a sense, dead." [139] What he points to here is the fact there is still an air of material, temporal certainty that remains within the JT framework, albeit non-intentionally and perhaps out of necessity given the context of the dominant culture.

All of this being said, within the JT movement there is recognition of these shortcomings and a growing articulation of deeper transition strategies under the rubric of, for instance, *solidarity philanthropy*[140] and *restorative economics.*[141] Social movements led by oppressed, marginalised and exploited peoples who have endured capitalist tyranny and may already be embracing some coordinates of post-capitalist realities are far further along than philanthropic institutions in creating action, ethics and principles commensurate with the second horizon. All of this has ushered in a growing call for deeper relationality and reciprocity between funders and grantees, especially where historically marginalised peoples are entrusted to make their own funding decisions about those resources that belong to them or the lands that were stewarded by them in the first place.

---

[139] Akomolafe (August 27, 2021)
[140] See Robinson, C. (May 9, 2021) for an articulation of how philanthropy pursues incremental reform within the existing paradigm, while speaking the language of systems change.
[141] See Buen Vivir Fund (September 29, 2021).

REFLECTION EXERCISE: WEALTH AS PROXY FOR POWER

...

For the purpose of this exercise, let us assume that material wealth (the accumulation and hoarding of large sums of money) is a proxy for power.

...

Reflect on the following questions:

- What does your relationship with wealth as power look like? How does it feel in your body? How does it manifest in your life?
- How does your relationship with wealth/power influence your ontology, how you see the world?
- What is most compelling in the *Just Transition* movement if we imagine wealth as a proxy for power? What are some limiting constraints?
- What would an *onto-shift* in the realm of wealth/power look like?
- Consider that the etymology of the word sacrifice is "to make sacred". How do you see the overlap of the sacred and sacrifice, especially as it relates to wealth and power?
- What would you be willing to sacrifice to reconstitute your relations with wealth and power?

ARTWORK ON FOLLOWING PAGE:
"YOU CAN'T SOLVE MONEY PROBLEMS WITH MONEY"
~ FEDERICO CRUZ ~

Through our synthesis so far we have identified four overarching structural shifts within JT philanthropy pushing to Horizon 2 transition pathways. We have listed some examples with respective organisations within each category as a starting place for discussion:

SHIFTING DECISION-MAKING FOR GRANT GIVING

- This includes establishing participatory grantmaking for activists and communities to direct funding (e.g. Baobab Foundation and the Phoenix Fund in the UK and the Kataly Foundation, Agroecology Fund and Solidaire in the US).
- Expanding flow funding and giving circles where activists and community organisers can disintermediate foundations and make direct grants to allies and community members (e.g. Be the Earth Foundation in the UK and the long-term work of Marion Rockefeller Weber in the US).

DEEPENING RELATIONSHIPS OF TRUST

- There is a growing call for "trust-based philanthropy" where there are longer-term organisational grants (as opposed to project grants) where grantees have the freedom and flexibility to conduct their work (e.g. Libra Foundation and the Whitman Institute in the US).

SHIFTING RESOURCES AND ENDOWMENTS FOR COMMUNITY SOVEREIGNTY

- Transferring assets to communities to self-determine and govern their own asset management (e.g. Seed Commons, Full Spectrum Capital, Chordata Capital, all based in the US).
- Setting up land trusts to democratically steward land for the sake of self-sovereignty (e.g. Soul Fire Farm and the Schumacher Center for A New Economics, based in the US).
- Creating community foundations in order for historically marginalised and Indigenous peoples to lead, manage and grant funds into their local communities (e.g. Amigos de San Cristóbal in Mexico and the Global Fund for Community Foundations).

- Developing integrated capital funds for communities, including access to interest-free loan funds, reparation funds and other innovative funding mechanisms (e.g. Southern Reparation Loan and People's Solar Energy Cooperative – both based in the US – and the global solidarity fund Buen Vivir).
- Funding cooperatively-led organisations and bio-regional cooperatives (e.g. The Sacred Headwaters Initiative in the Amazon, Cooperation Jackson in the US, and Alliance for Food Sovereignty in Africa; the NoVo Foundation in the US is creating a sustainable bio-region around Kingston in upstate New York).

SHIFTING TIME HORIZONS

- Spend-down foundations that use endowments to speed up the process of wealth transfer and reparations (Namaste Foundation, Christopher Reynolds Foundation, and Chorus Foundation, all based in the US).
- Blending endowment funds with grants to create more speed and flexibility in giving (e.g. ThirtyPercy in the UK and A Thousand Currents and Grassroots International, both based in the US).

We recognize that the JT movement is growing and evolving. What we have described here is not fully inclusive or exhaustive of its efforts, for instance, towards racial equity or decolonisation of philanthropy and NGO practices.[142] Still we want to draw attention to two interrelated observations. The first is that many of the efforts in Horizon 2 are pointing to a shift in understanding about wealth, how it should be distributed and who gets to decide this distribution. Taj James, the co-founder of Full Spectrum Capital Partners, told us: "People are starting to see that capital is energy that needs to flow like water. Water moves to the lowest places in geography. The places that require its flowing energy. Capital that is not flowing is simply the continuation of colonisation."[143]

---

[142] For instance, several groups are deeply engaged in funder-education efforts around JT transition pathways. For example, see the work of Justice Funders, Edge Funders Network, Thousand Currents, Grassroots International, Solidaire, Chordata Capital, and Movement Generation among others.

[143] James (July 10, 2021)

REFLECTION EXERCISE: INSTITUTIONAL DYING
(SPEND-DOWN VERSUS PERPETUITY)

- PAUSE -

...

Reflect on the following questions:

- What would happen if you and/or your organisation decided to close your operations within a given time period (e.g. five to ten years)?
- What feelings and thoughts come up? Do you feel constriction or a relief in your body?
- What do you think are the main drivers of your emotional and somatic response?
- How do you think your personal conception of and relationship with death affects your relationship with the perpetuation of institutional forms?
- What other thought-forms are intertwined with death for you (e.g. scarcity, control, identity, status, livelihood, obligation, etc.)?
- If you mapped your philanthropic work using the Three Horizons framework, where would a spend-down strategy be situated?

The second valuable insight in this regard is that there are very few pathways that are currently creating lived post capitalist possibilities within and towards Horizon 3. In our research, we observed a significant dearth of systemic alternatives outside of the usual neoliberal constructs.

To create pathways of possibility, we believe that a commensurate shift in ways of seeing, sensing, knowing and being in the world is also required. The logic that demands social justice is not necessarily the same logic that creates a world of interconnected, embodied justice. To use the language of Bayo Akomolafe again: "Demands for social justice may get us a seat at the table, but they will never let us leave the house of modernity."[144]

The JT articulation is an important contribution, and it is giving birth to something beyond JT – *Just Transition plus a commensurate shift in ethico-onto-epistemologies*. Since you probably won't share that term with your friends, we will call this *Justice Plus Onto-Shifts* (a slightly more communicable meme for a bar scene with a high geek ratio).[145] Essentially, we cannot create a just world without also shifting our understanding of knowledge itself (including why we think we know what we think we know), how we see & relate to the world, and how we ethically intra-act within the entangled universe.[146]

ARTWORK ON FOLLOWING PAGE:

"OTRA ONDA VIENE"

~ ALIXA GARCÍA ~

---

[144] Akomolafe (August 27, 2021)

[145] The language of *onto-shift* is borrowed from David Bollier and Silke Helfrich's book, *Free, Fair and Alive: The insurgent power of the commons*.

[146] In her book *Meeting the Universe Halfway*, Karen Barad writes about intra-action (as opposed to interaction) to illustrate how entanglement precedes thingness. In other words, there are not simply "objective things" that make up the world and interact, but rather, relational lines. It is more apt to say that ongoing relational dynamics are responsible for how things emerge. See Barad (2007).

BEYOND JUST TRANSITION: JUSTICE PLUS ONTO-SHIFTS

~

In many ways, *Justice Plus Onto-Shifts* has been the unstated rallying cry of Indigenous communities and social movements from the geopolitical South for decades. Such impulses are rooted in Indigenous, place-based, animistic, relational understandings of the world. They remind us that our existing and emerging alternatives must be rooted in a pluriverse of approaches.[147] The goal is to create, as the Zapatistas say, *un mundo donde quepan muchos mundos* ("a world in which many worlds fit"). This is part of the ontological shift we are gesturing towards.

If we were to play an acronym game, the *Plus* of *Justice Plus* could stand for: pluralistic, liberatory, uniting and symbiotic approaches. Pluralistic in the sense that they do not claim universality but rather honour simultaneous ontologies and cosmologies; liberatory in that its desired outcome is the liberation of all beings; uniting in that they create common ground between diverse groups of beings, human and more-than-human; and symbiotic in that they are Earth-based approaches focused on regenerative, reciprocal ways of being. This is what emancipatory movements that combine both a justice lens and a *onto-shift* approach are teaching us.

Groups such as the *Global Tapestry of Alternatives*, *Shikshantar*, *Local Futures*, *Universidad de Tierra*, the *Buen Vivir* movement, the *Zapatistas*, the *Rojava* experiment, the *Emergence Network*, and many others have been articulating the role of alternative epistemologies and ontologies as being core to social justice work. Autonomous communities such as *Comunidad de Paz San José de Apartadó* in Columbia and *Favela da Paz* in Brazil, and of course, the countless Indigenous communities that have been embodying onto-shifts and post capitalist realities for hundreds, and in some cases, thousands of years.[148]

---

[147] See *Pluriverse: A Post-development dictionary* by Kothari, Salleh, Escobar, Demaria, & Acosta (Eds.) (2019).

[148] This has also been key to the work of many of the writers and thinkers of the anti-colonialist and post-development movements, as well as Indigenous cosmologies, including Arturo Escobar, Chinua Achebe, Boaventura de Sousa Santos, Robin Wall Kimmerer, Vandana Shiva, Gustavo

Justice Plus Onto-Shifts mean *justice-as-ever-becoming* rather than being an idealised end, or a static state of a justice we can 'know'. We are gesturing towards a justice that requires both a dismantling of systems of oppression *and* a simultaneous shift in the ways we see & behave in the world, the manner by which we approach social change, and a shift in the very gaze by which we make sense of these changes.

Justice Plus recasts justice as a verb, not simply a noun. *Justice Plus* demands that we create designs and practices to address the root causes of our separation from the living world, within ourselves, our communities and the superstructures of the global political economy simultaneously and in perpetuity, with no final destination in sight.

Justice Plus requires us to actively sense and explore the depths of commodification, consumption and cannibalism that are born out of and perpetuate the dis-eases of modernity and money itself. These include the entitlements and virtues we believe money confers on the wealth holder (or, conversely, the beliefs in victimhood or scarcity often correlated with the absence of money).[149] *Justice Plus* asks us how we ourselves are benefiting from the existing order, and what we are willing to give up – not for sacrifice's sake, but as an offering to a living planet and all her inhabitants that are in deep relationality with us.

If we were to take this further, one could argue that *Justice Plus* invites us to prepare ourselves to communicate with the consciousness of wealth itself in order to embody and create an alchemical, transformational, paradigmatic shift. *Justice Plus* moves towards the possibility of an animate cosmos and perhaps even our ancestors or future beings (including ourselves) helping us learn to conceive an emerging grammar and a felt experience of other ways of knowing, sensing and being so we can begin to practise post capitalist philanthropy.

Esteva, Ivan Illich, Aime Cesaire, B.R. Ambedkar, Subcomandante Marcos, Abdullah Öcalan, Davi Kopenawa, Samir Amin, Gloria Anzaldúa, Fernando Huanacuni Mamani, Tiokasin Ghosthorse, Alberto Acosta, Ashish Kothari, Ariel Salleh, Vanessa Andreotti and many others.
[149] For a deeper look at the link between cannibalism and capitalism, see Forbes (2011) for the landmark text *Columbus and Other Cannibals* by Indigenous scholar Jack Forbes. Also see Ladha & Kirk (2016).

GRAPHIC ON FOLLOWING PAGE:
ONTOLOGICAL SHIFTS

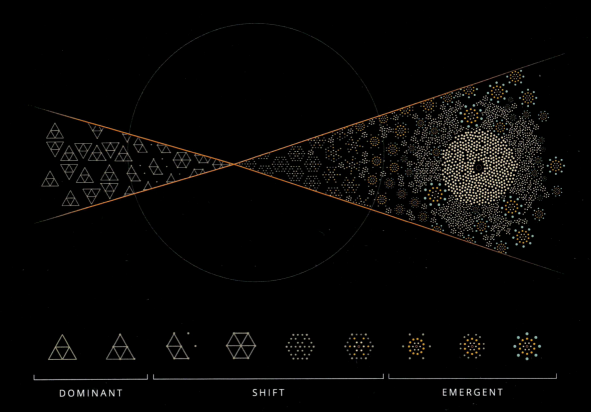

The notion of *continuum* is our starting place for mapping out the various transitions of the figure below. We are beginning to sketch out continuously emergent *Justice Plus Onto-Shifts*: transitions from binary logic to *continuum-ways* which incorporate practising, sensing, and embodying these shifts in order "to enact a multiplicity of interdependent temporalities".[150] Rather than a past versus present, old versus new, immanent versus transcendent dichotomy, the goal should be to enter a continuum of time in which "the past, present and future co-exist, interpenetrate and mutually implicate each other."[151]

> *Justice Plus invites us to prepare ourselves to communicate with the consciousness of wealth itself in order to embody and create an alchemical, transformational, paradigmatic shift. Justice Plus moves towards the possibility of an animate cosmos and perhaps even our ancestors or future beings (including ourselves) helping us learn to conceive an emerging grammar and a felt experience of other ways of knowing, sensing and being so we can begin to practise post capitalist philanthropy.*

CONTINUUM OF ONTO-SHIFTS

The movement from binary logic towards the continuum of *onto-shifts* goes beyond temporality, and has implications for issues as diverse as social organisation, the use of appropriate technology, relationships to the more-than-human realm, and gender & sexuality. We are moving towards more fluid, queer and non-conforming identities. Identity as contextually co-created across a spectrum rather than identity as fully-formed, pre-existing, permanent, and foundational. Below is an initial exposition of some relevant *onto-shifts* as they pertain to philanthropy and social justice more broadly.

---

[150] de la Bellacasa (2017) p.215
[151] Adams (2004)

CONTINUUM OF ONTO-SHIFTS

Rational logic	*Trans-rational logic*
Monoculture	*Polyculture*
Ahistorical amnesia	*Remembering, repairing, reconciliation*
Seperation, materialism, positivism	*Non-dual, animistic, queer, quantum*
Unquestioned orthodoxy	*Self/collective responsibility for first principles*
Attribution and competition	*Service and solidarity*
Accumulation of capital	*Liberation of capital*
Transactional	*Relational*
Entitlement	*Entrustment*
Bureaucracy	*Beauty*
Trauma	*(Re)cultivation of life-force*

This continuum, of course, requires a concomitant shift from the realm of traditional rationality (e.g. in which conclusions follow ordered premises) to a more trans-rational approach (i.e. approaches where rationality and logic sit alongside and are not prioritised over other ways of sensing, knowing & being and contextually integrates them as relevant layers of 'reality'). This allows us to incorporate felt experience, intuition, somatic expressions, the whisperings of ancestors, murmurings of wind, the received wisdom of plants and even surges of *metanoia* – spontaneous transformations of heart.[152]

As discussed in Part I, the directional logic of capitalism is towards monoculture: one totalising way of thinking and being, championed by global 'winners' and power elites imposing Euro-American values of individualism, efficiency, certainty, supremacy and domination. A core part of Enlightenment thought has been duality & separation, and its accompanying cosmology meant to dehumanise non-Europeans and "thingify" Nature (a necessary precondition for capitalism to flourish, as previously mentioned). Therefore, the antidote logic to this form of thought might be described as *polyculture*: acknowledging and honouring the many

---

[152] Metanoia is derived from the Greek word metanoiein, meta + noein to think, from nous or mind. It refers to a transformative change of heart or mind, often in relation to a spiritual conversion.

ways of knowing, sensing and being; the plurality of tongues and approaches; the "fugitive epistemologies" that will not conform to silos and parameters.[153] This embrace of polyculture can and must include our more-than-human relations, as we open ourselves to what the physicist David Bohm called the "implicate order", an omnicentric worldview connected to the wholeness of every perceived other.[154]

The dominant culture can be characterized by an ahistorical amnesia, dutifully unaware of the ongoing consequences and legacies of colonialism, enslavement, imperialism, genocide, patriarchy, violence, displacement and the other drivers of historical capitalism. It can also be characterised by the desire for novelty, innovation, and escape – the search for something *else, out there, in the future* – rather than the presence required for the uncomfortable and difficult task of restoration, repair and healing work, of "staying with the trouble", to borrow the language of Donna Haraway.[155] The antidote to this amnesia may ultimately be the very acts of remembering, the pathways for reparations, and the aim of reconciliation with not only other peoples, but with land, with Earth herself, and with our more-than-human kin.

A critical *onto-shift* here is the move away from the five-thousand year old cycle of separation and dominion over the natural world, and the three-hundred year old perverse Enlightenment logic of human exceptionalism. The reduction of the world to materialist principles and the belief in a positivist rationality where the world can be fully deconstructed and understood by the human mind are mere relics of scientism and colonialist hubris. What we are seeing emerging in all fields today – from quantum physics to Earth systems science, from behavioural economics to evolutionary anthropology – is a picture of the world that is non-dualistic, animistic, queer and quantum (with all its attendant laws of non-locality, entanglement, uncertainty, and observer-created phenomena).[156]

Central to our dominant culture is the unquestioned orthodoxy of both science and market fundamentalism. These are so deeply ingrained in us that to question these

---

[153] "Fugitive epistemologies" is a term borrowed from Bayo Akomolafe. See Akomolafe (March 11, 2020).

[154] Bohm (1980)

[155] Haraway (2016)

[156] Greene (2003)

logics – their efficiency, effectiveness, and overall supremacy – is tantamount to questioning a reigning monotheistic God; one becomes irrational in the eyes of all others. What we are seeing emerge through *Justice Plus Onto-Shifts* are new-ancient-emerging practices for individuals to take radical responsibility for themselves and their collective inquiries into the inner and outer cosmologies that govern our lives.

Rather than accepting the first principles that have historically been handed down by institutional religions, the state, the media and the high priests of science and the market, there is a renewed desire (and necessity) to deepen our understanding of the world, and our place within it as a spiritual-political praxis. By this we mean a process in which concepts may be enacted, embodied, and realised. This is not something only philosophers or mystics, Indigenous peoples or activists do. It is a requirement of being a citizen in troubled times, and especially for those of us who choose to hold responsibilities for the transition of unjustly-held wealth and power.

Central to post capitalist philanthropy is the move away from the desires for attribution (taking credit, needing to be named, seeking legacy) and competition that characterise the dominant form of philanthropy, to creating embodied cultures of humble contribution, reciprocity, service, solidarity and cooperation with all beings (human and otherwise) that are actually doing the work of our world. What we are starting to see is that big funders cannot simply give to organisations that pronounce values they arbitrarily deem important, but, rather, they must honour all beings entangled in the creation of new-ancient-emerging worlds.

This is directly tied to shifting our relationship with wealth from one of accumulation, hoarding, stockpiling, and then doling out, to one where we recognise the liberation of capital as an alchemical, entangled act affected by intention, attention, awareness, expectation, historical antecedents, and other factors. *JT Plus Onto-Shifts* also move away from transactional, commodified relationships between funders and 'grantees', or even money and outcomes, to a relational, interwoven fabric of interbeing.[157]

---

[157] Interbeing is a term coined by Thich Nhat Hanh in his important book, *Interbeing: Fourteen Guidelines for Engaged Buddhism*. The English word "interbeing" is an approximation of the Vietnamese *tiep hien*. *Tiep* roughly translates to "being in touch with" and "continuing." *Hien* roughly translates to "realising" and "making it here and now." As a doctrine, interbeing is interpreted as Buddha's doctrine of *Dependent Origination*, particularly within a Mahayana Buddhist perspective. See Nhat Hanh (1987).

This is a move from a culture of entitlement (e.g. I am entitled to these funds because of the work I do, my family lineage, etc.) to a culture of perceiving and honouring multiple entanglements, including living in appreciation of the entrustment of these webs of relations, where gratitude is the root of both receiving and giving gifts. As the cultural critic Lewis Hyde reminds us: "When gifts circulate within a group, their commerce leaves a series of interconnected relationships in its wake, and a kind of decentralised cohesiveness emerges."[158]

Although we are currently seeing some of these shifts occur, given the nature of bifurcation we are also witnessing an entrenchment of the dominant logic in both the broader culture and in philanthropy. As the state-corporate complex increases its bureaucracy, so do most large foundations (they have even strengthened their justifications to hold on to power and grow endowments as a counter-balance to the state-corporate complex). Simultaneously, there is a corresponding move to enchantment, enlivenment, and beauty. For example, there is a growing movement around *biomimicry* in architecture, design and urban planning where humans emulate the genius of Nature's designs and processes.[159]

Relatedly, we are seeing both an increase in the creation and amplification of the wounds of trauma culture and a (re)cultivation of life-force – our communal and self-healing capacities to regenerate our unsevered bond to the living world that in turn feeds and regenerates our abilities to survive and thrive within the neoliberal desert. We see an ever-growing awareness emerge of issues such as wellness, resiliency, and trauma within the philanthropic and social change sector. However, much of these efforts are aimed at supporting people to be more well-adjusted to their institutions and to capitalist modernity in general, rather than supporting any potential access to liberatory states-of-being.

This emerging continuum of onto-shifts is not a linear process; it exists in a multitude of ways simultaneously. It does not assume a linearity of time, but rather is a messy, involuted process of remembering and forgetting, striving towards and retreating from, creating new pathways and falling into habit again. Just as some of the initial sparks of the JT movement have been co-opted by the dominant culture of philanthrocapitalism, even shifts in ontology, behaviour, language and practices

---

[158] Hyde (2009), p.xxxvi
[159] Benyus (1997)

will likely be usurped and sold back to us as radical reform. As we alluded to above, we are in the depths of bifurcation, one may say these are part of the death throes of late-stage capitalism. There is, and will continue to be, both a simultaneous reaction and a calcification of dominant culture as new-ancient-emerging possibilities take root. Nevertheless, to unearth *contextually-relevant* pathways for transition, we must continue to practise and live *onto-shifts*, as if Life depends on it.

"

A critical onto-shift here is the move away from the five-thousand year old cycle of separation and dominion over the natural world, and the three-hundred year old perverse Enlightenment logic of human exceptionalism. The reduction of the world to materialist principles and the belief in a positivist rationality where the world can be fully deconstructed and understood by the human mind are mere relics of scientism and colonialist hubris. What we are seeing emerging in all fields today – from quantum physics to Earth systems science, from behavioural economics to evolutionary anthropology – is a picture of the world that is non-dualistic, animistic, queer and quantum (with all its attendant laws of non-locality, entanglement, uncertainty, and observer-created phenomena).

"

REFLECTION EXERCISE: PRACTISING *ONTO-SHIFTS*

...

- PAUSE -

...

This exercise will take about fifteen minutes and will require another person to practise with.

1. For the first part of this practice, please hold an object that has significance to you. It could be a stone, a watch, or a piece of jewellery. Something that feels familiar and holds a special meaning for you. Simply hold this object in your hand and feel its significance to you for a few minutes. Then contemplate how it came to be in your presence. How long did its constitutive parts evolve within Nature, or, if it's synthetic, how was it made? If it could speak, what would it say to you? What are its teachings? What would you say to this object if you saw it as a being or even as kin?

2. Right after the first meditation with your "object", find a place where you can face out into Nature. If you're in an urban environment, this could be a single tree or plant in your house or a vegetable. Then go through a similar contemplation whilst deepening your understanding of its significance, what it would say to you, what are its deepest teachings, and what you would say to this being.

3. Finally, sit in front of another human being, in silence. We would like you to stare into each other's eyes for about five minutes or so. You can ask similar questions in your internal dialogue without speaking aloud. Once the five minutes are complete, you can share with each other your experiences and the different textures of wisdom that came from the object, the living landscape and the human kin in front of you. Feel free to journal any insights that may come too.

REFLECTION EXERCISE:
CONTEMPLATING *JUSTICE PLUS ONTO-SHIFTS*

...

- PAUSE -

...

The art piece on the *next pages* was created by the Colombian-born visual artist and poet, *Alixa Garcia*.

The heartbreaking story of Rachid Mohamed al Messaoui's journey across the Strait of Gibraltar inspired the artwork. The Moroccan boy, age of 16, created a makeshift floater out of plastic bottles and bags to help him swim across the frigid waters to the Spanish coastal town of Ceuta in search of refuge. He was apprehended by border patrol and returned to Morocco shortly after.

Take some time with this piece. What do you think is happening in this scene? What aspects of the piece validate your beliefs and feelings about what you are seeing? Does the image remind you of something else? If so, what? Why do you think the artist offered this piece in relation to the onto-shifts? By contemplating this work, did you experience aspects of an onto-shift of your own? If so, how would you describe it?

ARTWORK ON FOLLOWING PAGE:
"FORCED MIGRATION AGAINST A GALACTIC EXISTENCE"
~ ALIXA GARCÍA ~

Flip the art piece to contemplate

PART THREE

FROM PYRAMID LOGIC TO SPIRAL LOGIC

FROM PYRAMID LOGIC TO SPIRAL LOGIC

~

"All has been consecrated.
The creatures in the forest know this,
the Earth does, the seas do, the clouds know
as does the heart full of love.

Strange a priest would rob us of this
knowledge and then empower himself
with the ability to make holy
what already was."

– St. Catherine of Siena, 14th century Christian mystic [160]

"The fall of Empire, gentlemen, is a massive thing, however, and not easily fought. It is dictated by a rising bureaucracy, a receding initiative, a freezing of caste, a damming of curiosity – a hundred other factors. It has been going on, as I have said, for centuries, and it is too majestic and massive a movement to stop."

– Isaac Asimov [161]

The first part of this book analysed the dominant culture of philanthropy through the lens of a nested hierarchy, where philanthropy, its various institutions and the individuals that comprise those institutions were shaped, sculpted and, in a critical way, determined by the bounds of neoliberal capitalism. Part II moved us from the realm of neoliberal paradox to the emerging possibilities being born from the JT movement, leading us to a continuum of *onto-shifts* within a broader framework of *Justice Plus Onto-Shifts*. We will now go deeper into the (re)cultivation of life-force, as well as the other attributes and aspects of the continuum of *onto-shifts*, as we move into the spiral logic of post capitalist philanthropy.

---

[160] Ladinsky (Ed.) (2009), p.199
[161] Asimov (2021), p.494

In this section, we will attempt to invert, disrupt and dance with the ordering of pyramid logic by rooting our inquiry within the womb of materialism; cosmology itself. As with all parts of the spiral, cosmology will continually be affected by, and with, all other constitutive parts in a multi-directional, reflexive, discursive, non-linear and interconnected manner.

We will then deconstruct & reconstruct the notion of the 'individual' in the midst of a spiral, acknowledging that we are all first moulded and entrained by a worldview that has been cultivated, socialised, honed, pruned and internalised over lifetimes of exposure to the dominant culture through individual experiences, familial and cultural legacies, inherited epigenetic phenomena, and other factors.

This embedment within a worldview or cosmology is also true for groups (what we call social ecologies), sectors (what we call biomes) and superstructures (what we call mycelial services). Just as our broader analysis must be rooted in the meta-container of a living planet, our analysis for potential pathways of transition must root (and unroot) the individual from the meta-beliefs and meta-masks that constitute identity. This is a perfect starting place for our dance with spiral logic.

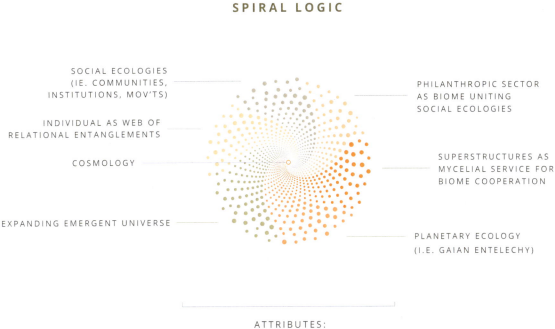

SPIRAL LOGIC

SOCIAL ECOLOGIES
(IE. COMMUNITIES, INSTITUTIONS, MOV'TS)

INDIVIDUAL AS WEB OF
RELATIONAL ENTANGLEMENTS

COSMOLOGY

EXPANDING EMERGENT UNIVERSE

PHILANTHROPIC SECTOR
AS BIOME UNITING
SOCIAL ECOLOGIES

SUPERSTRUCTURES AS
MYCELIAL SERVICE FOR
BIOME COOPERATION

PLANETARY ECOLOGY
(I.E. GAIAN ENTELECHY)

ATTRIBUTES:
MULTI-DIRECTIONAL, REFLEXIVE, DISCURSIVE, NON-LINEAR AND INTERCONNECTED

COSMOLOGY AS THE CENTRE OF SPIRAL LOGIC
~

"The use of philosophy is to maintain an active novelty of fundamental ideas illuminating the social system. It reverses the slow descent of accepted thought towards the inactive commonplace. If you like to phrase it so, philosophy is mystical. For mysticism is direct insight into depths as yet unspoken. But the purpose of philosophy is to rationalise mysticism: not by explaining it away, but by the introduction of novel verbal characterizations, rationally coordinated."

- Alfred North Whitehead [162]

Territory is more than just the environment, territory is our whole lives. Our body is the territory and the territory is our body. We should be thinking beyond politics, and think about how we can re-enchant the world again. Awaken our senses. The challenge is to reforest our hearts.

- Célia Xakriabá [163]

As mentioned earlier, it is important to note that we are not trying to replace one hegemonic worldview or framework with another. The spiral itself is simply one representation of infinite, fractal possibilities for nesting the inner and outer work of building post capitalist realities. We are seeking a rhizomatic container that allows for multiple, non-hierarchical entry and exit points for analysis and unfoldment. As stated above, the spiral connotes a multi-directional, reflexive, discursive, non-linear and interconnected approach to understanding and embodying our roles when intra-acting with the work/play of systemic change.[164]

---

[162] Whitehead (1968), p. 174

[163] Célia Xakriabá is an Indigenous educator and activist from the Xakriabá peoples of Brazil. This quote was shared through Culture Hack Labs (2021) in their support of the #CuraDaTerra campaign that Célia helps co-lead.

[164] As mentioned in Part II, in her book *Meeting the Universe Halfway*, Karen Barad writes about *intra-action* to illustrate how entanglement precedes "thingness" (i.e. there are not simply "objective" things" that make up the world and interact, but rather, relational lines). See Barad (2007).

The starting place for this work is the worldview or cosmology that we hold as individual, yet entangled, agents desiring social change. As we have stated before, ideology and meaning construction are always background conditions. If we are not conscious of the underlying structures of beliefs, we inherit the dominant beliefs of the cultures we are embedded within.

Through our interviews with practitioners in both philanthropy and social change we were surprised by the paucity of interrogation, reflection and contemplation that existed within the sector vis-à-vis the critical questions of what philosophers call "first principles" or what spiritual activists call "underlying consciousness". As one foundation board chair said to us: "I really don't know anyone in philanthropy I could have a conversation with about the big questions of why we are here, what we are doing and where we are going as a species."[165]

Academia (especially philosophy), religious institutions, nation states, the scientific community and other organs of traditional power have attempted to provide answers to these questions, with the result (intentional and otherwise) being a mass usurpation of the capability for deep reflection and an abdication of personal responsibility for ongoing sense-making. We are not suggesting answers to these questions; rather we would like to posit that within the context of the Anthropocene, anyone engaging in the work of deciding who will receive funding and resources must first grapple with the questions arising from first principles.

Before we move on to what individuals working or relating to the field of philanthropy can do, we ask the reader to first spend some time contemplating, sensing into and uncovering these first principles. They may seem unrelated to our lines of inquiry, or perhaps they may feel "too big"; however, we ask for the readers' trust. Our aim is not for any one being to answer these questions definitively, but simply for you to sit with them, to allow them to seep into your consciousness, to feel into your somatic responses, and to spend some time in bewilderment with them.

We will start, appropriately, with the realm of ontology. How do you define reality? What do you believe constitutes this reality? How does one accurately recognise reality? Do you believe that there is such a thing as objective reality or Truth? If so, what constitutes this Truth or Truths? Within the dominant culture, these questions

---

[165] Buffett, J. (November 26, 2021)

have been the historical domain of metaphysics, existentialism and the philosophy of science.

How much of your conception of reality has been shaped by the religion you have been most closely affiliated with (including atheism, if relevant)? How much of your conception of reality has been shaped by a scientific-materialist worldview? If you had to respond without citing scientific precedent, how would you respond to this question: why do you believe human beings exist? How did we get here? What is our purpose, if any, for being alive? What is our relationship to the Earth and the more-than-human world? What is sacred to you? Why? How do you define sacredness?

What is the origin of the universe? Do you believe in the Big Bang theory? Do you believe that humans can know the answers to these questions? If you do believe in the scientific consensus, why do you believe in it? Have you conducted inductive or deductive analysis yourself? What have you concluded from your research and contemplation? What still remains unanswered and unexamined for you?

Some questions that traditional institutions and modes of thought rarely consider, but we ask that you do, include: what does the more-than-human world tell us? How does non-human consciousness (e.g. plants, animals, bacteria, rocks, fungi, lichen, protozoa) perceive reality? How can we know what other intelligences are communicating to each other and to us?

Can one cultivate the ability to listen to plants, animals and other kin? Can we receive messages from ancestors or even unborn progeny? Do you believe there could be extra-physical layers to reality? What do you think and feel when you hear the term "Spirit" or "God" or "consciousness"? What do they mean to you? If there are realms or dimensions of reality that we cannot (or do not yet) know, what does this tell us about reality?

From there, we can move into the realm of epistemology, or the study of knowledge. What can we truly know? How do we know what we think we know? What are the bounds to human knowledge, cognition and perception? What if science is only a limited, partial worldview filled with limiting assumptions which may be better categorised as the *floor of understanding* rather than *the ceiling* (i.e. the cumulative, pinnacle knowledge of all of humanity)? What does the more-than-human world have to tell us about matters of knowledge? How can we even conceive of knowledge we may never know or understand?[166]

> *Our aim is not for any one being to answer these questions definitively, but simply for you to sit with them, to allow them to seep into your consciousness, to feel into your somatic responses, and to spend some time in bewilderment with them.*

What is beauty? Where is it derived from? Is it universal? Is it hard-wired into human cognition? How much of our conception of beauty is socially constructed or defined? How much do we avoid what we deem not beautiful? This is the traditional domain of aesthetics, an under-appreciated branch of philosophy that seeks to better understand our relationship with how we define, perceive, judge and sense the world.

What is morally just? What is considered good behaviour and bad behaviour? Why do we deem it so? In some ways, the areas of moral philosophy are most pertinent to philanthropy. Who deserves funding and why? Why do people who have accumulated wealth through a particular system have disportionate power to decide on the livelihoods of those who have not benefited from this system or have actively been harmed by it? How do we decide which issues deserve attention and which can be ignored? Such questions have traditionally been the realm of ethics and theology.

What is your conception of power? How should power be distributed? Who gets to decide how resources are distributed? Who gets to decide on who gets to decide? We have inherited many of our ideals around political philosophy from the dominant worldview of liberal, capitalist democracies stemming from Ancient Greek & Roman thought, and European Enlightenment conceptions of power. What other types of power are we ignoring? What are the other ways for decision-making to happen? What are the potential structures outside the nation-state model?

Of course, hundreds of thousands of people, maybe millions, have spent lifetimes over the past five-thousand plus years contemplating and debating these types of questions. There are no right answers and there is no amount of time that will allow us to arrive at any 'final answer'.

---

[166] Nagel (1974)

We are not asking you to answer these questions once-and-for-all.

These are questions to live and walk with. Approaching them requires humility, uncertainty and, often, the request for support. We suggest you ask such questions often, and in communion with nature, and then to simply listen. Your 'answers' will invariably reflect partial, temporary notions that will continue to change and evolve through ongoing application.

Making your beliefs explicit, at least to yourself, is a critical step in building pathways to adjacent possible futures. As James Baldwin famously said: "Not everything that is faced can be changed, but nothing can be changed until it is faced."[167] The corollary of this is that not everything that is changed in the realm of ideas is changed in the realm of the body. Political-spiritual praxis is on-going work that requires addressing the contradictions between belief, actions, ethics and embodiment.

Part of what we are being asked to confront in the midst of the meta-crisis is how much of our understanding of the world, and even our understanding of how we understand it, is shaped by ideas we do not necessarily believe in or even fully understand. This part of the *paradox of performance* or *the paradox of culture* that we presenced in the opening section. We often perform and embody the values of the dominant culture we live in, even if we are critical of it and/or do not identify with it.

This is partly why thinking about how we think, often referred to as *meta-cognition*, helps us further develop our inquiries. Also, the practice of embodied cognition, of feeling how and where the ideas and language live and travel through our bodies, tracking their *somatic biographies*, can help to deepen the practice of decolonisation at the physical level.

Our worldviews determine our relationship with ourselves, with each other and with the living planet. They are being continuously woven and refined with each interaction. They make up an invisible web of beliefs, patterns, practices, dialogues, mannerisms and etiquettes that determine the ever-present event horizon. They are the becoming of our beingness, and the being of our becomingness.

---

[167] Baldwin (1962)

We are trying to *uncover* rather than *determine* our inherent and biassed ethico-onto-epistemologies in order to continually re-calibrate them in more *contextually-relevant* ways. As we unearth and reflect on our responses, beliefs and actions, our ethics are often revealed. When we contemplate our ethics, our contradictions are often revealed. Ethics is not separate from our understanding of how we understand or why we are doing what we are doing. For example, if the philanthropic sector cares about the preservation of life, ecology, and reducing suffering, there exists an ethical dilemma and contradiction in continuing to provide and grow endowments through capital markets, as well as directing the vast majority of funds to "solutions" for the symptoms rather than root causes, while simultaneously exacerbating the root causes.

Most people rarely contemplate what they believe, even more rarely consider why they believe what they believe, and many rarely discuss these matters of utmost importance in the realms of work, especially in the world-making areas of social change and philanthropy. Donna Haraway articulates this beautifully when she says, "It matters what matters we use to think other matters with; it matters what stories we tell to tell other stories with; it matters what knots knot knots, what thoughts think thoughts, what descriptions describe descriptions, what ties tie ties. It matters what stories make worlds, what worlds make stories."[168]

---

[168] Haraway (2016), p.12

REFLECTION EXERCISE: FIRST PRINCIPLES OF COSMOLOGY

...

– PAUSE –

As we suggest above, spend time in reflection and contemplation with these questions. We recommend gathering in a triad to discuss. This should be a trusted group of three or more colleagues that can provide a powerful canvas and mirror to deepen your inquiry. As you reflect on and walk with these questions in the days ahead, both alone and/or with your small group, notice how these questions may be relevant in your day-to-day life.

- Where in your body do you feel each question? Can you track which part of your body your initial responses come from?
- What have you uncovered about your ethico-onto-epistemology? What does this point to about how inner thought forms (e.g. scarcity, fear, control, generosity, solidarity) shapes your cosmology and orientation in these times?
- Identify and reflect on a few examples of where your beliefs, ethics, and actions are congruent or contradictory. What does this illuminate about how you live and make decisions?
- Go for a walk outside in a place you find beautiful and peaceful.
  Reflect on the following questions:
  - What actions do you take that affirm your cosmology? What actions negate it and indeed may contribute to harm?
  - What does a life-affirming cosmology mean to you?
  - As you walk, pause now and then to notice the quality of your thoughts, your breathing, your bodily responses, your visual field, your sense of sound, smell and taste.
  - Is it challenging to be in perception and sensation simultaneously (e.g. do your thoughts distract you or get quieter or louder)?
  - What type of cosmology do you hold in your work life? Is this cosmology consistent with your actions?

ARTWORK ON FOLLOWING PAGE:

"NATURE IS A CONDITION OF EXISTENCE"

~ FEDERICO CRUZ ~

INDIVIDUAL BEINGS AS WEBS OF RELATIONAL ENTANGLEMENTS

~

"It would be best to consider this as a continuing 'revolution of consciousness' which will be won not by guns but by seizing the key images, myths, archetypes, and ecstasies so that life won't seem worth living unless one is on the transforming energy's side."

- Gary Snyder [169]

"I belong to those whose hearts are broken for my sake."

- Sufi proverb

As we move from pyramid logic to spiral logic, we enter the web of relational entanglements. Individuals are, of course, not separate beings in the sense that capitalist modernity asserts. We are messy spillages of interactions, encounters, ancestors, bacteria, the foods that nourish us, the lands that hold us, the love that binds us, just to name a few interdependencies.

Dorion Sagan reminds us how biologically interdependent we truly are:

> *Ten percent of our dry weight is bacteria, but there are ten of 'their' cells in our body for every one of 'ours,' and we cannot make vitamin K or B12 without them. Vernadsky thought of life as an impure, colloidal form of water. What we call 'human' [is] also impure, laced with germs. We have met the frenemy, and it is us ... Indeed, we literally come from mess-mates and morphed diseases, organisms that ate and did not digest one another, and organisms that infected one another and killed each other and formed biochemical truces and mergers.*[170]

---

[169] Snyder (1974), p.101
[170] Sagan (November 18, 2011)

In a few personal conversations before he passed, the philosopher and activist Gustavo Esteva reminded us: "We can believe we are individuals, we can feel as individuals, think as individuals, but we cannot be individuals. We are knots in nets of relations."[171] Karen Barad explains this deep entanglement in terms of quantum field theory, as the ongoing dynamic of emergence that constantly reconfigures us: "Entanglements are not intertwinings of separate entities, but rather irreducible relations of responsibility. There is no fixed dividing line between 'self' and 'other', 'past' and 'present' and 'future', 'here' and 'now', 'cause' and 'effect'."[172]

Similarly, there is no fixed dividing border between our inner and outer worlds. That is, the individual interacting in the world is also in inextricable relational entanglement with the inner structures – the soma, emotions, thoughts, ego, and cultivated states of being (e.g. equanimity). The realm of soma includes trauma; histories carried in our cells (ancestral, familial, bacterial); current states of health or illness; how much time we are sedentary or active; the emotional states that our bodies traverse through in any given moment; the epigenetic phenomena that were experienced by our ancestors and a host of other factors we cannot fully know. These inner states and structures are in a dynamic relationship with each other and the so-called outer world, blurring the lines of entanglement even further.

We presence these facts to situate human beings as more-than-individuals, to invoke the sense of intra-being and interbeing that comes with the queering of the classical world of Newtonian physics and Cartesian demarcations. What is our responsibility as more-than-individuals, while being non-dualistically incarnated in a seemingly single corporeal body? How do we best tend to our intricate relational lines, both seen and unseen? What does it mean to be in solidarity with so-called others?

There are no neat and tidy answers to these questions, no frameworks of lucidity that we can offer the reader. Rather, we merely suggest five avenues for exploration and inquiry into relationality: [173]

---

[171] Esteva (August 26, 2021)

[172] Barad (2010), p.265

[173] Some of these ideas have been adapted from "What is Solidarity?", see Ladha (2020).

1. **Becoming a good student of the dominant culture**

    For one to understand power, one has to understand culture. In order to decode culture, one must develop critical faculties. To be critical, one must disidentify with the object of critique, in our case, the dominant culture.

    We spend inordinate amounts of time consuming "culture", yet we do not necessarily have the means to cultivate a deeper understanding or critique of culture. The anthropologist Clifford Geertz believed that "the human is an animal suspended in webs of significance that we ourselves have spun."[174] Indeed, culture is the cumulation of these webs of significance. It is only by unveiling the threads that we can start to grasp the limitations of our perceived reality in the attempt to expand the horizons of possibility. In other words, *onto-shifts* require that we understand what we are shifting from and what we are shifting into.

2. **Decolonising the mind-body-heart-soul complex**

    This requires a de-colonisation of one's entire being. As we have stated before, this is a continual praxis of deconditioning old constructs of greed, selfishness, short-termism, extraction, commodification, usury, disconnection, numbing and other life-denying tendencies of the dominant culture. This also requires re-educating our mind-body-heart-soul complex with intrinsic values such as interdependence, altruism, reciprocity, generosity, cooperation, empathy, non-violence, interbeing and solidarity with all Life. Our loyalty is not pledged to an individual foundation or a (dead) donor's legacy or a sector; our fidelity is to the living world.

    To do so requires taking responsibility and relinquishing power. The geographer and philosopher Katherine Yusoff reminds us that the "attempt to absolve the positionality of Western colonial knowledge and extraction practices, while simultaneously reinforcing and resettling them in a new territory – a Western frontier of pioneers armed with eco-optimism and geoengineering – indicates a desire to overcome coloniality without a corresponding relinquishing of the power it continues to generate in terms of who gets to formulate, implement and speak to/of the future."[175] Undoing this will require a perpetual practice of decolonisation.

---

[174] Geertz (1973), p.5
[175] Yusoff (2018), p.27

> *For one to understand power, one has to understand culture. In order to decode culture, one must develop critical faculties. To be critical, one must disidentify with the object of critique, in our case, the dominant culture.*

3. **Making values explicit; linking cosmology, care and creation**

   As we deepen our critique of the dominant culture, we will naturally start to oppose the values that are rewarded by our current order. By better understanding what we stand against, we will deepen our understanding of what we stand for, to cue our dear Osiris, whose journey we opened this text with.

   As we create intimacy with ideas, practices and embodiments that cultivate solidarity, empathy, interdependence and other post capitalist values, we also refine our internal world, the felt experience of what it is to be a self-reflective, communitarian being in service to Life. As we shift internally, we may find the external world of consensus reality starts to mirror back these values, and, in turn, our bodies will reflect the external changes.

   It is a common belief that there is an oppositional relationship between inner work and outer work, spirituality and politics. They are seen as separate domains – politics happens in halls of power or the streets, and spirituality happens in ashrams, churches, temples, forests, caves and other places of worship. This separation is often manifested in statements such as: "I have to take care of myself before I can help others". This notion overlooks the possibility that being in service to others can be the driver of self- and communal transformation, which, again, affects the self. By linking our cosmologies, care and acts of creation, we can transcend the traditional binaries of internal versus external evolution.

4. **Creating embodied cultures of lived possibility**

   Part of the practice of resistance to dominant culture is to create and live alternatives of such beauty and extraordinariness that the so-called 'others' are magnetically drawn to post capitalist possibilities. As part of this, we must enact spiritual-political praxis with others in community and in dialogue to create embodied cultures of change and lived possibility.

   The word 'spiritual' is loaded for many, and has multiple meanings and associations. The reason we use the word in this context is to distinguish between the materialist, Newtonian aspect of reality as the 'seen world' and gesture towards a more quantum, Bohrian aspect of the unseen and unknowable as also real. We are invoking the aspect of 'spirit' that speaks to the infinite potentiality of the world of the formless, in addition to aspects of reality that we do not yet understand (and perhaps never will) including consciousness itself.

   The idea of a spiritual-political praxis also nods to the life-force energy that lives at the nexus of our inner landscapes and the material conditions we face in the world. We are interdependent with our social and ecological contexts and the liberation of internal life-force requires a constitutive restructuring of our material realities. The enclosure of the wider social and ecological context is partly how and why capitalist modernity has been able to sever our connections with our ancestral past and has actively created and reinforced trauma in our bodies.

5. **Practising emergence**

   Emergence is not just a concept or a metaphor – it is a state of being. It is also part of a spiritual-political praxis, and the ability to understand and navigate it can be learned. Emergent phenomena have certain attributes that are based on context, cultivating the conditions and containers for change, letting go of control or perceived control, iterating as complexity adapts, deep listening, and even deeper humility. Emergence is an antidote to hubris. Emergence is also interdependent with the observer (or witness). How we perceive phenomena, including ourselves, and the archetypal role we are playing when we are observing intra-actions, informs how and what emerges.

We are being prepared for even deeper complexity, breakdown, tragedy, renewal and rebirth. This transition calls upon all of us to be vigilant students of our cultures, to contemplate our entangled destinies, to abandon our perceived entitlements, to transcend the apparent duality of inner and outer work, to create embodied cultures, to practise emergence, and to reaffirm our responsibility to each other and the interwoven fabric of our sentient planet and the living universe.

The more we can cultivate our connection (and notice our resistance) to life-force, the more we may be able to change the superstructures around us and inner structures within us, the more we can inhabit the immediacy of the present moment, and so on. The skill of being present with what is, while creating what could be, allows us to access the deep grief that comes with being a human in the Anthropocene and potentiates the generosity of spirit that is required to flourish in these times. This does not mean anything will become easier; rather, we simply have the opportunity to become more learned in "staying with the trouble."

> *Emergence is an antidote to hubris. Emergence is also interdependent with the observer (or witness). How we perceive phenomena, including ourselves, and the archetypal role we are playing when we are observing the intra-action, informs how and what emerges.*

REFLECTION EXERCISE:
SEEING AND WEAVING RELATIONAL ENTANGLEMENTS

...

— PAUSE —

Practices for relationality as identity:

Becoming a good student of the dominant culture

Decolonising the mind-body-heart-soul complex

Making values explicit; linking cosmology, care and creation

Creating embodied cultures of lived possibility

Practising emergence

...

DOMINANT — SHIFT — EMERGENT

As we start to reflect on the new-ancient-emerging beliefs, values and the *onto-shifts* required, we would like you to reflect on the following questions:

- How do you practise being a good student of your culture? One way is to spend some time reflecting on the connection and consequences of your material footprint in the world. Please consider:
    - Do you know where your waste ends up? How far can you trace it?
    - Look around your physical environment. What energy and resources are you aware of that you are currently using? Where are the energy and resources extracted from? If you do not know, how can you find out? Why might this be challenging?

- Where and how is your food grown? How did it get to you? Where does your water come from and who is dependent on the same watershed?

- What are the dominant cultural narratives you see in the world around you (e.g. in films, songs, media and rituals such as weddings)? How are the dominant cultural narratives in your community formed, and who shapes them? Who or what spreads them? What does the dominant culture reveal (reinforce, alter, expand, etc) about your beliefs or ontology?
- How does your spiritual orientation inform (or not) your political beliefs and behaviours?
- What are some methods or practices available to you (that you have learned, from your lineage, or spiritual tradition) that allow you to step out of self-identity and perceive yourself as a web of relationships?
- How do you understand and practise emergence? Who do you know that is well-versed in the practice of emergence? What questions would you ask them to deepen your own practice?

INSTITUTIONS AS MEMBERS OF SOCIAL ECOLOGIES

~

"There are no hierarchies in nature other than those imposed by hierarchical modes of human thought, but rather differences merely in function between and within living things."
- Murray Bookchin[176]

"When we are dreaming alone it is only a dream. When we are dreaming with others, it is the beginning of reality."
- Dom Helder Camara

Just as we have reconstituted individuals as webs of relational entanglements, we can also reconceive institutions as enmeshed webs of relational entanglements which we refer to as social ecologies. The term *social ecology* was coined by Murray Bookchin in his seminal text *The Ecology of Freedom* where he states: "The very notion of the domination of nature by man stems from the very real domination of human by human."[177]

We are not simply taking a normative stance to say that philanthropy 'should' be organised along the lines of non-hierarchical, interdependent social ecologies, as Nature is. Rather, we are taking an observational stance to say that philanthropy is already enmeshed in social ecologies, currently based on domination. However, these relational ecologies, and their consequences, are not acknowledged.

Philanthropy is embedded in a social matrix that includes relationships with grantees, civil society, social movements, communities-of-practice, the natural world, the land upon which participants live and work, the watershed, unseen forces, capital itself with all its historic antecedents, fossil fuels, the global economy, and so-called 'affected communities', to name just a few. As we recast individual

---

[176] Bookchin (1986), p.486
[177] Bookchin (1982), p.1

institutions as constitutive members of social ecologies, we are supporting an *onto-shift* towards a more relational-interbeing worldview that can hold the complexity, interdependence and multi-directionality of such intricate entanglements.

The *onto-shifts* that would both be required, and would discursively result, from asking and living into such questions would be an ecosystemic approach to relationality and a deeper relationship to place. We would acknowledge that we are literally ecosystems through our external and internal relationships, including the land we inhabit and work on. On a cellular level, we are made up of communities of bacteria and microorganisms. There are ten bacterial cells in our body for every cell of 'our' bodies[178]. On a temporal level, our ancestors are living through us, as are future generations of our lineage, if they have the same chance at life as we did. On a spatial level, we are an ecology of selves, of all the beings, seen and unseen, that we are in perpetual entanglement with. Our relationality defines us.[179]

Perhaps philanthropy would not seek tax breaks (i.e. foundations would pay local taxes, not set grants against income, not use opaque donor advised funds, etc.), nor would it see itself as a separate sector worthy of these exemptions. As a social ecology, the impulse would be to nourish the land, its neighbours, its community, reconcile with the Indigenous peoples upon whose territory they occupy, contribute their share of support to public services and divest from equity markets. Here, philanthropy would be embedded in right relationship, living into reciprocity.

Another shift might be philanthropic institutions recasting their primary objective to *spend-in* financial endowments towards the creation of post capitalist infrastructure (e.g. bioregional infrastructure to ensure land, water, food, health, medicine, cultural and educational sovereignty for local communities), support ecosystems of social movements, cultural interventions, and wisdom traditions that help dismantle exploitative systems.[180]

The idea of spend-in builds on the traditional philanthropic concept of spend-down (or spend-out) where a foundation essentially spends its endowment funds, in addition to its 5% grant-making allocation, usually into its existing portfolio of

---

[178] MacDougall (2012)

[179] A version of this argument was first made in Ladha (2019).

[180] We are grateful to Andrea Panaritis for creating and sharing the concept of *spend-in*.

grantees. We are suggesting a spend-in that may or may not bear resemblance to the existing set of giving practices and the current portfolio. It flips the logic and power from "it is ours to spend-down in the ways and timelines we decide upon" to "this is our reparative work to spend-in towards our collective and ecological healing".

One of the most innovative and biomimetic approaches we found in our research came from a UK foundation[181]. They plan to spend-down their endowment in relation to the golden ratio, or the *Fibonacci sequence* i.e. their annual spending will be a percentage of their endowment determined by the sum of the percentages spent in the two previous years. This will allow them to build upon lessons from the previous year and to liberate their capital within a period of eleven years (having given away 1% the first year). In an interview with CEO Jen Hooke, she commented that this golden ratio model is, "the opposite of how investment currently works. In investment, returns are cumulative. We will be distributing in reverse."[182]

> *On a cellular level, we are made up of communities of bacteria and microorganisms. There are ten bacterial cells in our body for every cell of 'our' bodies. On a temporal level, our ancestors are living through us, as are future generations of our lineage, if they have the same chance at life as we did. On a spatial level, we are an ecology of selves, of all the beings, seen and unseen, that we are in perpetual entanglement with. Our relationality defines us.*

If the foundation distributes 1% of its endowment in the first year, it would then double to 2% in the second year and then to 3% (adding 1% and 2%) for the third year. The fourth year would be 3% plus 2% for 5%. Year five would be 5% plus 3% for 8%. Year 6 would be 13% (the previous year's 8% plus 5% from the year before). Year 7 would be 21%. This is where it starts to get interesting. Year 8 would be 34%. Year nine would be 55%. Year ten would be 89%. And then whatever funds are remaining would be distributed in year eleven.

---

[181] Thirty Percy Foundation, UK
[182] Hooke & Mowll (July 14, 2021)

In conversations with Matthew Monahan, co-founder of the Namaste Foundation based in the US, he suggested the idea of a "cascading commons" amongst foundations.[183] Essentially what this would mean is that, as one foundation agrees to spend-in its endowment, another foundation, with the capacity for more grant-making, would agree to cover the difference in grants that would result from the reduced endowment for the period of the first foundation's *spend-in*.

One of the main reasons foundations resist traditional spend-downs is that their annual grant-making is usually reduced by this measure, negatively affecting their grantee partners. By creating a commons pool amongst funders, some foundations can more easily spend-down without affecting their grantee partners, and the collaboration amongst these foundations can support more net spending into broader social ecologies.

Such applications of spiral logic can create potential practices that embody post capitalist values. There are multiple, growing avenues to this, including community-led grantmaking, giving circles, flow-funding, asset and land transfers back to communities, and other means of reparative, restorative, participatory funding in order to build the required infrastructure and governance practices required to live outside of a dominant culture.[184]

None of the ideas outlined above are ends in themselves, but, rather, practices in letting go of control, creating contexts of direct democracy, and activating currently atrophied muscles. They embody a transition from *transactional giving* to *relational giving*. Transition is not an end-state. It is a journey of un-learning, experimentation, re-learning, integration, humility and then unlearning all over again. By definition then, transition is emergence.

---

[183] Monahan (July 7, 2021)
[184] For a comprehensive set of resources see Indie Philanthropy Initiative (October 14, 2014).

REFLECTION EXERCISE:
SEEING PHILANTHROPY AS WEBS OF RELATIONS

- PAUSE -

...

We offer some intentionally provocative questions to contemplate and stimulate a shift in philanthropy's gaze towards webs of relations – a social ecology. As you read these questions, notice which ones you more easily engage with and why.

- First take 5-10 minutes to make a web of your relationships. What role does giving or receiving funding play in your relational web of interdependencies?
- What if philanthropists started to proclaim that the world's wealth is all of our collective endowment & inheritance, and that the burden of deciding who gets what should be shared as part of our collective healing, restoration and repair of right relationships?
- Consider what it would look like for a large portion of your funding to be decided by a circle of allies and practitioners (rather than by boards, senior leadership, or wealth-holders). What would letting go of control in this way feel like? How would you ideally structure decision making within this web of relations?
- What if we considered concentrated wealth as a disease of the body politic, manifesting in personal and communal dis-ease, that can only be addressed through collective, reparative redistribution through gifting?
- What if we started seeing the role of philanthropy as the healing, alchemisation and liberation of capital, rather than the notion of money as something to be preserved and grown for security, power, status and ongoing wealth?

PHILANTHROPIC SECTOR AS BIOME UNITING SOCIAL ECOLOGIES

~

"We feel insecure, paranoid even, because all the other outcomes we can see require the implosion of the house we inherited but live in fear of losing. Let's put our creative and critical capacity to use making some colourful parachutes to slow the fall, turn it into something exciting and edifying… Where do we go to design parachutes? We go to that place beyond this hard Earth: the land of dreams. Not of dreams as we usually speak of them when we wake up from a nap, or the kind we banalise in the sense of "my dream job" or "my dream car". I mean dreams as the transcendental experience in which the human chrysalis cracks open onto unlimited new visions of life."

- Ailton Krenak, Brazilian Indigenous activist and philosopher[185]

"The task, on the contrary, is to recognise that the seeds of a community ethic – and, indeed, of benevolence – still exist. It is to join up the remnants of local culture that survive, and give it the chance to get its confidence back. We now need to move from a precious interest in culture as entertainment, often passive and solitary, to culture in its original, earthy sense of the story and celebration, the guardianship and dance that tell you where you are, and who is there with you…"

- David Fleming[186]

As we move from the hierarchical, exploitative relations of pyramid logic to the biomimetic approach of spiral logic, we will continue the ecological metaphor of expanding circles of relationality. As social ecologies represent assemblages or groupings of beings, human and otherwise, that share interests, intentions, interdependencies, and other entanglements. These assemblages are contained

---

[185] Krenak (2020), pp. 62-64
[186] Fleming & Chamberlin (Ed.) (2016), p.50

within the geographic area of a biome. (A biome is a large area characterised by the similarity of its terrain including its vegetation, soil, climate, and wildlife).[187]

Rather than thinking of philanthropy as a 'sector', a neoliberal understanding of a grouping of disparate, competing organisations that sell or provide a similar commodity or service, and therefore have similar interests, the notion of a biome provides a more holistic, integrated approach to organising around shared principles, processes and outcomes. Biomes exist on a continuum of health depending on the wellbeing of the vast constituencies and ecologies that make up the terrain of the biome. Think of a mycelial network in its vastness, intelligence, and communications across a habitat. We find this is a useful metaphor for an emerging approach towards post capitalist philanthropy.

What if the purpose of philanthropy was to serve as a biome to unite the various social ecologies that are entangled within its orbit (from grantees to movements to financial advisors to family members)? What if the aim of the biome was to create a context for restoration, transformation and the (re)cultivation of life-force, both internally and externally?

If capital is both a poison and a medicine, how do we transmute capital to render it benign, and potentially even beneficial for healing? How do we use capital in the short window of time left where capital is 'useful' and accepted as a means of organising human labour, time and priorities while acknowledging its destructive nature and historical tendencies?

What if capital does not want to be compounded or stockpiled to serve a few? What if it wants to flow and circulate freely to serve the biome, the collective commons? In conversation with the authors, Gopal Dayaneni stated: "The transition of philanthropy has to do with the capacity of social movements to build; to be able to turn the inward flow of investment from philanthropy… and return it to the commons."[188]

Like social ecologies, at a higher fractal scale, biomes operate with shared goals, intentions, and desired outcomes. These are not necessarily planned or organised

---

[187] National Geographic (September, 22 2020)
[188] Dayaneni (November, 19 2021)

in a traditional sense; similar to other complex, adaptive systems, the outcomes are emergent, non-linear and generative from the values that define the inputs of the system. If philanthropy is money thrice stolen, as Colin Greer suggests, and if money cannot solve the problems that money has created, what would post capitalist philanthropy look and feel like?

> *How do we use capital in the short window of time left where capital is 'useful' and accepted as a means of organising human labour, time and priorities while acknowledging its destructive nature and historical tendencies?*

What if the aim of post capitalist philanthropy was to disintermediate our collective dependency on capital? Throughout our interviews, we often heard the notion that the role of philanthropy should be to put itself out of business. Or at the very least, given our current context and crises, take this idea seriously and take bolder, more expedient steps in this direction. What does this look like in practice? Quite simply, it is a world in which the debt/growth model of capital is challenged at its root. At a macro-economic level, philanthropy would champion what ecological economists called *de-growth* – refocusing the global economy to be about well-being and the flourishing of Life rather than measuring GDP growth as the prime metric of success.

Currently, capital mediates all aspects of our lives – from where we live to what we do for work to what we do with our leisure time to what food we have access to and beyond. It seems only appropriate that we disintermediate ourselves from the grips of life-destroying capital and the globalised supply chain of extraction and exploitation.

FIVE ELEMENTS MANDALA

~

What does the transition to disintermediate capital look like? To rephrase this question, how do we use capital to create and support post capitalist realities? Let's start with three concepts mentioned above: *restoration, transformation and the (re) cultivation of life-force.*

Like all terms, they can mean many things and have connotations that are generic or banal. In order to attribute more than words, we will build out a visual map of how and why these three aspects can work together as a critical force for reconstituting the biome of philanthropy.

Our "coordinates of possibility" will take the form of a *mandala* (Sanskrit for "circle"). In Hinduism and Buddhism, mandalas are believed to represent different aspects of the universe. They also represent a spiritual journey from the external world to the spiritual centre. In Chinese medicine, for instance, mandalas can be used as healing guides and maps to show imbalances, relational dependencies, and alchemical journeys towards wholeness. They can also be used to focus the attention of practitioners as instruments of meditation and reflection.

Our mandala starts with a focus on the two intersecting axes – the vertical and horizontal lines of action. The X axis represents *Restoration and Solidarity* with the lens of addressing historical injustices while rebalancing and recentering right relationships. We focus on restoration not as some idyllic Palaeolithic state, but as a return to a symbiosis with the living world, a re-integration of humanity into the broader congress of Life (i.e. acknowledging that we ourselves are Nature, not an elite species that sits upon some kind of natural hierarchy) and an acceptance & integration of multiple simultaneous ontologies. It includes a temporal lens informed by historical harms, by what can be done now, and the requisite *onto-shifts* required to do so in both the present and future to reconcile and integrate the past.

Some of the questions we sit with as we explore this terrain include: How do historical antecedents play themselves out in the capitalist present? How do we incorporate approaches that potentially include reparations on the one hand and regeneration of ecosystems and reciprocal relational lines on the other? How do we approach in ways that do not replicate the colonial ontological lens that would perpetuate harm while believing we are practising solidarity?

The Y-axis represents *Transformation and Creation* with a focus on building and catalysing new-ancient-emerging ways of living, knowing, sensing and being. We must have a point-of-view on the shortcomings and pathologies of the dominant culture to know what kind of transformation we are seeking and we must also have a felt sense of what energies need to be rebalanced and cultivated for creation, for the state change of transformation to occur. Simultaneously, we also need a point-of-view and lived praxis for how to change or nurture emerging life-centric cultures and lived possibilities.

Let's start with the X-axis, which focuses on living in right relations with historically marginalised peoples as the relational vector of the biome. On the left hand side, we start with solidarity and support for the Indigenous peoples and communities of the planet who continue to responsibly steward human relations with our non-human kin and their living ecosystems.

Of course, Indigenous peoples are not a monolithic category of people. They are as varied and diverse in their cultures, practices, cosmologies, histories, geographies, contexts, and approaches as are non-Indigenous peoples. What many of them share is that, despite 500 years of colonial slaughter, exploitation and pillage, their communities have preserved the *wisdom of place* and relationship to land; generational, symbiotic knowledge of their respective terrains that continues to be necessary for human survival. We also acknowledge that many Indigenous peoples have survived the brutality of capitalism, have faced various collapses and disruptions, and are often already living in a continuous terrain of post capitalist realities. In many ways, they are among the best placed to lead us in the current and coming transitions.[189]

---

[189] Rushworth & Jamail (2021)

WATER

SOLIDARITY WITH
INDIGENOUS PEOPLES

The right hand side of this axis represents social movements, especially movements from the geopolitical South – the majority world in terms of living human souls. These are groups and peoples who are directly affected by the onslaught of neoliberalism, and are historically and currently dehumanised as their lands and bodies carry the most valuable "resources" to the life-destroying machine of capitalism. As Kathryn Yussof reminds us in *A Billion Black Anthropocenes or None*, the so-called Anthropocene "is an inhuman proximity organised by historical geographies of extraction, grammars of geology, imperial global geographies and contemporary environmental racism. It is predicated on the presumed absorbent qualities of black and brown bodies to take up the body burdens of exposure to toxicities and to buffer the violence of the Earth."[190]

These groups continue to risk their lives, organising with their communities to resist current power structures, to revive and grow mutual aid and solidarity networks, all while preserving and connecting to their ancestral ways and lands. Again, this is not simply about historical reparations in a financial sense. Although this is a necessary aspect of the healing of money, on its own, it is insufficient. Funding and being in solidarity with social movements is also about listening to, responding, honouring and learning from the needs of the peoples and lands that modern wealth has been built on, without their consent.

---

[190] Yusoff (2018), p.xii

FIRE

SOLIDARITY WITH
SOCIAL MOVEMENTS

The *Restoration and Solidarity* axis represents reparations, reconciliation, reciprocity and regeneration in the ongoing endeavour to incorporate a historical, structural lens and relational ways of being into our approach. It is about an ongoing practice of *onto-shifts* to perceive and offer from a place of relationality and reciprocity, rather than charity or aid. It is critical that accumulated wealth is spent-down, spent-in and spent towards the projects and alternatives that stem from deep time and local knowledge.[191] It is about rebalancing power in the places most affected by the ravages of capital and to promulgate ideas that could horizontally spread, in *contextually relevant* ways, to other bio-regions.

> As Kathryn Yussof reminds us in A Billion Black Anthropocenes or None, the so-called Anthropocene "is an inhuman proximity organised by historical geographies of extraction, grammars of geology, imperial global geographies and contemporary environmental racism. It is predicated on the presumed absorbent qualities of black and brown bodies to take up the body burdens of exposure to toxicities and to buffer the violence of the Earth."

[191] Recent research has shown that social movements are one of the most effective levers for combating climate change through their resistance to extractive practices. See Thiria, Villamayor-Tomásad & Scheidela (May 2022).

We began our mandala with restoration, as many healing modalities teach that energy must be restored before we can change states or heal. That is, *restoration is a necessary precondition for transformation*. And of course, transformation can facilitate restoration.

We will now move to the *Transformation and Creation* axis, which focuses on creating and living new-ancient-emerging cultures and expanding the collective imaginary.

AIR

CREATE NEW-ANCIENT-EMERGING
CULTURAL CONTEXTS

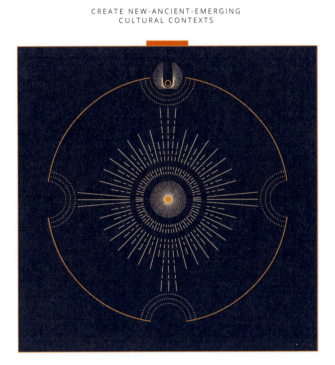

In order to address the root causes of our cultural disease of cannibalism and consumption, the post capitalist approach to philanthropy aims to expand the *Overton Window* of what is considered possible. This is a sociological concept referring to the window of potential, imaginable change the public deems acceptable and desirable, and therefore what culture-at-large is willing to include in discourse.

In order to do this, we must centre other ways of knowing and being, feeding polyculture, including more integral cosmologies that focus on the relationality and reciprocity between humans and the interdependent web of Life. We must engender the cultural context with compassion, empathy, service, generosity and solidarity while deepening our structural and constellational worldview. In some ways, this is the most difficult task of not only the philanthropic biome but the more robust social change biome. This will require practices of de-schooling, re-imagining, and re-tooling simultaneously. It requires an ongoing relationship with death and rebirth, renewal and the mysterious alchemy of transformation.

> *We began our mandala with restoration, as many healing modalities teach that energy must be restored before we can change states or heal. That is, restoration is a necessary precondition for transformation. And of course, transformation can facilitate restoration.*

EARTH

CREATE POST CAPITALIST
INFRASTRUCTURE

At the bottom of the Y-axis we focus on creating post capitalist infrastructure. This is the physical, cultural and societal infrastructure necessary to live outside the constraints of modernity, including the globalised, industrial supply chain. Essentially, the aim is to create systems and infrastructure for strong, resilient localised economies, deep democracy, community sovereignty, alternative modalities for health and education, flourishing ecosystems, and vibrant communalism.

We can see how these four vectors can overlay with their respective four elements – Indigenous peoples as the element of *Water*, the tributaries and veins of the planet; social movements as *Fire* blazing the way and bringing our attention towards life-centric alternatives through direct experience and place-based wisdom; seeding and building post capitalist infrastructure as the *Earth* element, as world-making; and creating and breathing into existence new-ancient-emerging cultural contexts as *Air*, re-animating and reconstituting the oxygen (i.e. ideas and consciousness) we breathe.

Then there is the critical work of healing the traumas of capitalist modernity and centering our relationship with life and death. This is the *(re)cultivation of life-force*, both internally and externally, restoring and revitalising the energetic weave and weft of living systems that has been perpetually denigrated by the onslaught of capitalism, commodification, violence and alienated labour. We are constituting life-force here as the element of *Ether* – the invisible, ineffable, ever-present force required for Life itself and for creative, vibrant evolutionary change.

We are not referring to the healing and (re)cultivation of life-force as some kind of neat, tidy end-state that is the result of therapy or medicine, but an on-going project of attending to the wounds of surviving the Anthropocene. This includes composting aspects of ourselves and our cultures that no longer serve us. Another relevant metaphor is cement removal – literally, figuratively, and somatically. Freeing the stuck and frozen parts of our bodies and developing our capabilities to connect with the currents of life and death.

Ether looks to approaches that can reconstitute our body-soul-heart-mind complex, unblocking the currents of life, stitching together perceived separate, fragmented selves back to wholeness. *Ether* can also be seen as an attunement, a subtle listening or perception, an opening to wonderment & mystery, and accessing the healing powers of the living world. Life grows in the dark, in the womb, under the frozen lands of winter. We aim to give space to the reconciliation of shadow aspects, to unacknowledged traumas, to the awe of mysteries that may be as diverse as gravity and light.

There is an old saying in psychotherapy: "That which we do not heal in ourselves, we transmit to others." Many of us continue to observe how our personal and collective wounds persist through the binary, oppositional politics of social justice activism as well as in philanthropic problem-solving. Even the most progressive movements deepen the project of othering, often as an explicit tactic to build support around a constituency (e.g. the 99% versus the 1%). We ourselves have often been found guilty of this practice as a way of mobilising people on issues we have deemed important.

> *Then there is the critical work of healing the traumas of capitalist modernity and centering our relationship with life and death. This is the (re)cultivation of life-force, both internally and externally, restoring and revitalising the energetic weave and weft of living systems that has been perpetually denigrated by the onslaught of capitalism, commodification, violence and alienated labour. We are constituting life-force here as the element of Ether, the invisible, ineffable, ever-present force required for Life itself and for creative, vibrant evolutionary change.*

We will not be able to create and live life-affirming cultural modes, memes, mores, ethics, etc. without healing the source-code of trauma that we have internalised from the logic of the dominant system. As our colleagues at *Culture Hack Labs* argue, what is required are *syntropic frames* and related *embodied practices*.[192]

Syntropy is the opposite of entropy. Syntropy is about coalescing, healing divides, bridging worldviews. Syntropic frames dissolve oppositional binaries by creating relations of interdependence and interbeing."[193] For example, the frame, "Our healing is bound together", is an example of a syntropic frame because it does not create a separate, hierarchical relationship (i.e. one person being dependent on another) but a horizontal relationship of two (or more) equals whose healing can only occur by the other also receiving healing.

Of course, new-ancient-emerging cultural narratives and contexts will become more possible as more people create and live in communities of care with post capitalist infrastructure, secure to say what they believe and build from a place outside of material subjugation and need, without fear of repercussion from the dominant systems that reward othering, disconnection, obedience, and dominator behaviour.

Relatedly, when Indigenous elders and social movement leaders have the safety, security and solidarity necessary to sustain their ways of life and actively continue to create and build alternatives to the *live-work-consume-die* paradigm of capitalist modernity, lived possibilities can be more cultivated, amplified and shared more widely.[194]

We also acknowledge that capital alone will not solve the problems of capital. In fact, giving funds to many local communities or social movements in the absence of deeper practices to transmute financial capital into other forms of capital (relational, natural, etc.) and the requisite *onto-shifts* can exacerbate many existing conditions and create new problems. This approach is not aimed at isolating problems and prescribing solutions. This *Five Elements mandala* is not suggesting what to fund; rather we intend to offer a broader, holistic framework for philanthropy to reflect on, refine, iterate, contextualise, practice and remix.

---

[192] Culture Hack Labs (2022), About Page
[193] Culture Hack Labs (December 2, 2020)
[194] The concept of the *live-work-consume-die paradigm* is borrowed from the philosopher Hakim Bey (aka Peter Lamborn Wilson). See Bey (2003).

Moreover, we recognise that the idea of supporting certain groups of people may not be relevant in particular contexts and/or providing traditional capital may not be the antidote required for moving beyond transactional mindsets. Preeta Bansal, a former senior actor in the US governmental and corporate sectors, and an anchoring member of *ServiceSpace*, a global volunteer ecosystem committed to growing relational and multiple forms of non-financial capital, said in an interview with the authors: "We may need to think about money as fertiliser, where small amounts may help create useful starting conditions for composting traditional mindsets and dying systems, but too much may crowd out or impede the cultivation of other necessary forms of non-transaction-based capital that are essential for true transformation, including social, cultural, spiritual, community and energetic capital".[195]

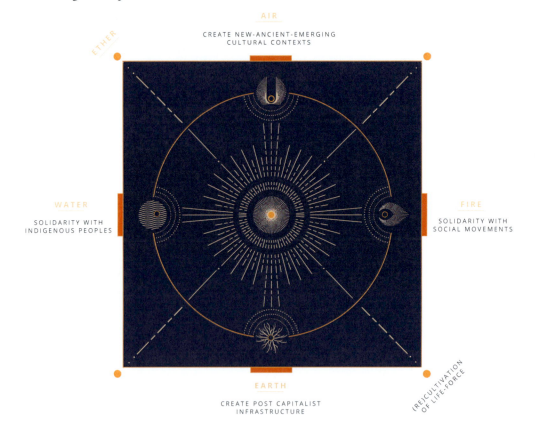

---

[195] Bansal (November 9th, 2021)

The notion of healing may mean different things in different cultural or historical contexts, and especially in reference to different types of capital. What is required for post capitalist philanthropy is both a structural worldview that includes an understanding of historical antecedents, ongoing practices and experimentation, and the constituent *onto-shifts*, recasting our perception and gaze.

The proposed *Five Elements mandala* is not a linear framework or any kind of final answer, but a discursive and emergent approach. We are offering a starting point for discussions on how social change could take form and what transition pathways could look like. The seed proposition is that if we approach philanthropic giving as a spiritual-political praxis that is bound to healing (including our own, with attention towards karmic implications), perhaps biome-level, life-affirming alternatives will emerge.

As we have discussed above, spiritual-political praxis refers to the connection between the inner and outer worlds. You can imagine the spiritual as the realm of psyche/soul/spirit – in other words, the inner life. Thus, political praxis is our way of seeing the outer/phenomenological world. In other words, of noticing how the material structures of power and identity affect our realities. We will delve into examples of each in the next section.

> *The seed proposition is that if we approach philanthropic giving as a spiritual-political praxis that is bound to healing (including our own, with attention towards karmic implications), perhaps biome-level, life-affirming alternatives will emerge.*

FIVE ELEMENTS MANDALA

ETHER

AIR
CREATE NEW-ANCIENT-EMERGING
CULTURAL CONTEXTS

WATER
SOLIDARITY WITH
INDIGENOUS PEOPLES

FIRE
SOLIDARITY WITH
SOCIAL MOVEMENTS

EARTH
CREATE POST CAPITALIST
INFRASTRUCTURE

(RE)CULTIVATION
OF LIFE-FORCE

KEY

RESTORATION & SOLIDARITY

TRANSFORMATION & CREATION

REFLECTION EXERCISE:
EXPLORING THE FIVE ELEMENTS MANDALA

...

Although this particular rendition of the Five Elements mandala is a biome level approach, with the desired outcomes of Restoration/Solidarity, Transformation/Creation and the (Re)cultivation of Life-Force, it can also be applied at the level of the individual, the institution or, as this section detailed, the superstructure.

...

Here are some questions for you to write and contemplate:

- What axis and elements would you include in your mandala? What does this Five Element mandala bring into focus? What is missing? What aspects do you disagree with or reject?
- What is your point-of-view on the fifth element of (Re)cultivation of Life-Force?
- How do you see and experience what we call Ether? How does life-force relate to your cosmology, your embedment in a web of relations, social ecology and biome?
- If you were creating your vision of a post capitalist future, what practices, policies, principles, projects, social movements, narrative interventions, etc. would you support within each element? How would you go about this work, and where would you start?
- What paradoxes would you have to embrace? How is this related to, or distinct from, your current areas of support and ways of working and being? Why?

SUPERSTRUCTURE AS MYCELIAL SERVICE FOR VARIOUS BIOMES

~

"I have come into this world to see this:
the sword drop from men's hands
even at the height of
their arc of
rage
because we have finally realised
there is just one flesh
we can wound."

- Hafez, 14th-century Sufi mystic[196]

"This is the hardest time to live, but it is also the greatest honour to be alive now, and to be allowed to see this time. There is no other time like now. We should be thankful, for creation did not make weak spirits to live during this time. The old ones say 'this is the time when the strongest spirits will live through and those who are empty shells, those who have lost the connection will not survive. We have become masters of survival – we will survive – it is our prophecy to do so."

- Tiokasin Ghosthorse, Lakota elder and cultural activist[197]

Now that we have established an experimental approach to the role of the philanthropic biome, the next nested spiral is the superstructure itself, the scaffolding for post capitalist realities. How do we create the contexts for multiple simultaneous ontologies, cosmologies and superstructures?

---

[196] Ladinsky (Ed.) (2002), pp 159-160
[197] Quoted in Coppola (June 30, 2010)

How do we move from the machine metaphor of the operating system to seeing the political economy as a mycelial service function, facilitating cooperation amongst the various biomes, including philanthropy, the nation-state (if such entities exists in the post capitalist world of your imagination), community-led and stewarded infrastructure, mutual aid networks, religious/spiritual organisations, solidarity networks, social movements, and civil society (among others).

Given that superstructures operate as complex, adaptive systems, part of our task is collectively to decide what designs, rules, values, norms, mores and other source material will potentiate emergent, generative properties. This can be done at an organisational, community and bio-regional level, or perhaps even at a larger scale.

Since undertaking such a vast collective process of creating shared cultural imaginaries is beyond our current scope, we will highlight our own subjective values, principles, approaches and objectives in our own desires for possible post capitalist possibilities to extend one iteration of the *Five Elements mandala*. We will also make suggestions for how the biome of philanthropy can support our suggested, subjective pathways to post capitalist realities.

Some key aspects and values for an emerging mycelial superstructure (i.e. a post capitalist, trans-local political economy) should include (but not be limited to) the following:

- Creating and supporting local, bio-regional sovereignty. This does not mean there would be no government, per se, but rather, the role of the state would be to de-evolve power to the level of lived experience (i.e. local communities and bio-regions that can self-govern).
- Promoting practices that build the currently atrophied muscles of community and citizenship in the web of life, including direct democracy, citizen's assemblies, co-operative ownership, community decision-making and commons stewardship, as tending to the web of social, ecological cultural relations.

- Re-calibrating notions of 'work' and 'value' to focus on the (re)cultivation of life-force and symbiosis with the natural world to create a spiritual/cognitive/creative renaissance for human and more-than-human flourishing.

- Preparing for coming changes through the preservation of life-centric ways of being, including diverse cosmologies, cultures, geographies and languages.

- Assisting an ecological transition for an adaptation to new environmental contexts.

- Synthesising the best aspects of capitalist modernity (we are not anarcho-primitivists and nor do we idealise an Edenic past; we are open to the idea that there are some things worth preserving and continuing) with the best of human nature (as understood through other contexts, from Palaeolithic cooperation and creativity to surviving Indigenous cultures)[198]. Some have called this merger between past, present and future, the creation/remembering of Ancient Futures.[199]

- Cultivating deeper humility, reverence, curiosity, and wonder as driving forces for post colonialist, post patriachal, anti-racist and post anthropocentric thinking and embodiment.

- Honouring the fractal nature of reality by promoting practices of inner-outer mirroring so that the work we support also supports deeper onto-shifts and a deeper intimacy with the living world.

- Embracing other ways of knowing and being, including (and especially) animistic and fugitive worldviews that allow for a deepening of new-ancient-emerging onto-ethico-epistemologies.

As we build one version of the *Five Elements mandala*, we are attempting to provide illustrative examples of the types of projects and programmatic areas that may help fulfil the desired outcomes above. These examples are not exhaustive, nor are they necessarily 'correct'. They gesture towards a type of philanthropy that could support bringing each element to life. Also, we have decided not to highlight sample organisations, as this would limit the imagination, create biases and we would invariably omit important contributions.

---

[198] See Graeber & Wengrow (2021) for a sense of the varied possibilities by which humans lived in cooperative equilibrium in extremely different historical and geographical contexts.
[199] Norberg-Hodge (2000)

As stated above, a core strategy and imperative of post capitalism is to use capital to build post capitalist infrastructure to facilitate bio-regional sovereignty, deepen symbiosis with the natural world, prepare for the coming shifts in global ecology, and to liberate our life-force for healing. We will start with the element of *Water*, representing solidarity with Indigenous peoples.

Work in this area can include funding and aligning with land and water protectors, food/land/water/medicine/cultural sovereignty projects, indigenous sciences, resistance movements, the *Rights of Nature*[200], legal jurisprudence, elders/wisdom circles and supporting the Life Plans[201] and the myriad efforts led by Indigenous communities that preserve and uplift their self-determination.

---

[200] "Rights of Nature is a short-hand term for a form of ecological governance that both provides for and prioritises Nature's right to flourish. It also provides for various subsidiary rights, such as the right to restoration, the right to its natural processes, and the right to ecosystem functioning without interference." See Zhongming, Linong, Xiaona, Wangqiang, & Wei (2019). We recognise that this work is based on the rule of law in securing and guaranteeing these rights. Yet, we still see promise in this work in that it acknowledges the sovereignty of the more-than-human world.

[201] Life Plans is a commonly used term amongst Indigenous peoples of the Amazon although the concept is used in other regions with different terminology. See Gaia Amazonas (June 8, 2020).

On the right-hand side of the *Restoration and Solidarity* continuum we have the element of *Fire*, with a focus on being in solidarity with social movements. Some of the most critical economic alternatives can be found amongst these groups, as they condense the lived experience of oppression whilst living and embodying other ways of knowing and being that in many cases already exemplify a state of post capitalism.

In terms of a few initial examples within the Fire element, this is where the philanthropic biome can nurture the social ecologies focused on issues such as:

- **Economic justice** – This includes de-growth & post-growth economics, universal basic income, a global wealth tax, abandoning GDP, the abolition of tax havens, a living wage, a shorter work week and universal basic assets including healthcare, alternative modes of education, and other issues.

- **Commons justice** – Infrastructure and policy that supports things such as co-operative ownership structures, the right to community spaces etc.

- **Freedom of expression** – This includes preventing extra-judicial killings, the right to protest, and other traditional human rights issues.

- **Democracy** – Including alternatives such as direct democracy and citizen's assemblies.

- **Racial justice** – Dismantling systemic racism and engaging in reparations and reconciliation work.

- **Food/land/water/medicine/cultural sovereignty** – Bio-regional self-sufficiency and support for movements, especially those facing agri-business interests, the World Bank and other encroachers of the commons.

- **Labour issues** – Including support for trade-unions and worker-owned cooperatives.

- **LGBTQI rights** – This includes the gender justice movements more broadly.

- **Education issues** – This includes both alternative education and "alternatives to education."[202]

---

[202] This term is borrowed from the late Gustavo Esteva, founder of Universidad la Tierra in Oaxaca, Mexico.

- **Migration rights** – This will become increasingly important as the climate catastrophe worsens and the traditional nation-state unravels. This work may include the abolition of borders and even ultimately the nation-state altogether.

Our argument is not that every foundation must support all of these issues; rather, as part of the project of supporting adjacent possibilities, we must aim to create a more equitable world where power and wealth are collectively redistributed, not as an end point, but a means to create a spiritual, creative, cognitive renaissance on the planet. Imagine a world where everyone is freed from the toil of "bullshit jobs"[203], and one in which local organising infrastructure can protect local cultural self-determination and bio-regional ecosystem integrity. These are necessary preconditions for desirable, emergent futures.

The root of the *Transformation and Creation* axis is the element of *Earth*, which is the necessary task of creating post capitalist infrastructure. By this we literally mean the physical, energetic, spiritual and cognitive groundwork that moves people outside of dependency on the globalised, industrial supply chain, and the underlying modernity logics that drive such extractive and destructive ways of living.

---

[203] Graeber (2018)

The *Earth* element also includes work on ecological restoration, land regeneration, and aligning into a just relationship with the more-than-human realm. It is where we practise ourselves out of our anthropocentric ways of imposing our demands onto the Earth, and instead listen and live in dialogue with the Earth and all of her inhabitants.

EARTH

CREATE POST CAPITALIST
INFRASTRUCTURE

EXAMPLES

ENDOWMENT AND OTHER FUNDS SUPPORT
BIO-REGIONAL INFRASTRUCTURE AND SOVEREIGNTY

RESTORATION AND PROTECTION
OF THE LAND AND PEOPLES

COMMON-BASED LAND STEWARDSHIP

MUTUAL AID NETWORKS

ALTERNATIVE COMMUNITIES, EXPERIMENTS,
AND TEMPORARY AUTONOMOUS ZONES

ALTERNATIVE CURRENCIES

OPEN-SOURCE KNOWLEDGE SYSTEMS

The *Earth* element includes, but is not limited to, supporting commons-based land stewardship (including creating local land trusts); alternative communities (and other experiments "outside the grid"); mutual aid networks; alternative currencies; open-source knowledge systems for locally tailoring decentralised models of production and consumption; ecological restoration and protection; and bio-regional resiliency and sovereignty (including work involving land, water, food, energy, medicine, health, education, cultural regeneration and sovereignty).

The focus here would be to not only use grant money (which traditionally can only go to not-for-profit organisations) but to use endowment funds as well to *spend-in* to, for example, gifting bio-regional infrastructure. This includes the more obvious domain of land, but also includes the requisite infrastructure needed for food, education, health-care alternatives and cultural sovereignty. This could then be managed cooperatively, especially by historically oppressed groups that have been displaced and dispossessed by capital (and the four horsemen of the apocalypse: imperialism, colonialism, genocide and enslavement).

The approach here is then to develop the atrophied muscles of local governance; to contribute to the restoration of the land and peoples (through reparations, regeneration, reciprocity and reconciliation work); to develop alternatives to existing extractive and dehumanising systems of healing and learning (i.e. health care and schools); to steward and protect water and forests; to promote localisation in production, consumption, and livelihoods; and to ensure that those who survive the deepening ecological emergency represent the diversity of humanity.

We see this work as essential to our collective futures. If the only humans that survive civilisational collapse are empowered elites who live within gilded walls, in bunkers or on private islands with submarines, the human enterprise would have failed, in our humble opinion. What is required is deep diversity, including a plurality of onto-ethico-epistemologies, languages, cultures and perspectives. This may seem like a bold and even outlandish claim, but we will not defend it here.

On the other side of the *Transformation and Creation* continuum is the element of *Air*: supporting new-ancient-emerging cultural contexts. In addition to creating the post capitalist infrastructure, we must also shift our cultural conditions, the memetic landscape of beliefs, and our dominant ontologies and cosmologies in order for emerging alternatives to take root and flourish. Given the contextual and place-based nature of this work, it is important to note that culture change work is extremely hard to propagate. It may be less the engine of the *onto-shift* and more of a *context cleanser* to make the environment less toxic and to help prepare the conditions for the change. We must open up spaces to create, imagine, and dream together.

This is the realm of artists, poets, culture hackers, shamans, educators and others. Here we include supporting cultural narrative work; artistic and creative interventions; emerging media approaches; sacred activism (work that goes beyond the binaries of traditional activism to include prayer and other trans-rational approaches); gatherings and other ways of accompanying and deepening relations (which are often not seen as a viable programmatic areas in and of themselves but are critical to nurturing a connective/relational fabric); and even the work that disrupts the philanthropic sector itself.

EXAMPLES

AIR

CREATING NEW-ANCIENT-EMERGING CULTURAL CONTEXTS

The final element is *Ether: (Re)cultivating Life-Force*. As we have discussed, this is especially critical because neoliberalism is an onslaught against our reproductive and regenerative abilities to heal and participate in the continuum of life and death. The perpetual trauma-inducing context of struggling to survive the spiritual desert must be countered by an equivalent or greater resurgence of life-force energy. The thought-form and experience of individuation and separation thwarts us from experiencing and connecting to the swelling currents of life that move through us and all around us in each moment.

In some ways, this is the most difficult element for which to give examples, as there are infinite paths into the work of healing and connecting to Life, all of which are highly subjective and must be contextually determined. We recognise that some of the modalities may be perceived as focused on individual healing; regardless, we are including a broad umbrella for *Ether* as we don't know what will crack us open, or what could transform our being.

ETHER

(RE)CULTIVATION OF LIFE-FORCE

RECONCILIATION AND RESTORATION CIRCLES

FAMILY CONSTELLATIONS, TRAUMA, AND SOMATIC-BASED THERAPIES

ANCESTRAL HEALING WORK

PHYSICAL EMBODIMENT PRACTICES
MEDITATION AND CONTEMPLATION

RITES OF PASSAGE WORK

PLACE-BASED SPIRITUAL PRACTICES
(SUCH AS THE LAKOTA INIPI OR SWEATLODGE)

CULTIVATION OF PERSONAL AND COMMUNAL CREATIVITY

RESURGENCE OF MYSTERY SCHOOLS

NATURE-BASED EDUCATION;
GRIEF CIRCLES AND OTHER COMMUNAL RITUALS

PSYCHEDELIC MEDICINES ESPECIALLY
THOSE ROOTED IN TRADITIONAL CULTURES

Some examples include: reconciliation and restoration circles; family constellations, trauma, and somatic-based therapies; ancestral healing work; physical embodiment practices, meditation and contemplation; rites of passage work; place-based spiritual practices (such as the Lakota Inipi or Sweatlodge); cultivation of personal and communal creativity; supporting the resurgence of mystery schools; nature-based education; grief circles and other communal rituals; and working with psychedelic medicines (especially those rooted in traditional cultures with the skillful means for true healing, such as Amazonian shamanic traditions).

Again, with all of these practices, it's critical that we do not replicate the coloniser's approach of consumption and acquisition, which keeps us locked in egoic, self-centred states of asking only "what I can gain" from this experience. We not only recommend the support and accessibility of these modalities for practitioners, but especially for *wealth holders* and *wealth granters*. Just as all oppression is connected, all healing is interconnected. The deepening of inner practices by all who are affected by and entangled in the murky, complex world of social change (especially social change that requires money) must continually strive to heal, integrate and reconnect themselves and their awareness to the present moment and the continuum of life.

The centrality of Ether pertains to how it directs our attention to the centrality of the body at various levels – individually, communally, institutionally, politically, culturally and in other ways. Just as science and Occidental thinking tries to reduce the world to the atom, and then splits the atom into the proton, neutron, electron, photon and so on, modernity also tries to reduce the body to its cells, mitochondria, DNA and other constituent parts. The element of *Ether*, as we are using it here, is a nod to the irreducible mystery of the body as a fractal whole of the world, and indeed, the universe. It requires approaching the body with awe, humility, reverence and compassion. The body is not a problem to be solved, but a mystery to be tended to through a practice of attunement, acknowledgement and integration.

The scaffolding of the *Five Elements mandala* is a starting place for contemplation, inquiry, practice and action. As we have seen, it requires the development of a cosmology at its heart, values that animate it, and practices that give expression to how it could be developed. To complete our iteration of the *Five Elements mandala*, we will add a final layer of lived practices. Again, we include how philanthropy can support and embody the lived practices for (re)cultivating life-force in service to post capitalist realities.

We recognise here that philanthropy can and often does change *what* it does. However, if it does not change *how* it behaves, the motivational landscape and how it sees the world (i.e. the requisite *onto-shifts*), we will inevitably replicate the same structures we are attempting to change. Several times throughout this text we refer to the importance of inculcating and practising other ways of being, sensing and knowing. What we haven't yet touched on are some of the known practices which philanthropy could more consistently adopt so as to shift power, support emergence, and ultimately bring about the transformation of the sector in these troubled times, which may include eventually rendering institutional philanthropy obsolete – i.e. hospicing philanthropy.[204]

Some of these practices are well known, some are part of a growing call to decolonise philanthropy, some have been highlighted in Part II of this book when we discussed the *Just Transition* movement, and some are more experimental. For the sake of simplicity, we here highlight a few indicative practices.

Our starting place is granting long-term, flexible, general operating support to organisations, social movements and communities. Long-term would mean providing grants for a minimum of five years, and up to ten years. Flexible, general operating support means allowing organisations, movements, and communities to lead and determine the work, scope, strategy, budget decisions, and trust in them to do so. We also suggest providing funds to groups beyond those formally registered as not-for-profits, even if it means creating entirely new mechanisms to do so.

Another critical practice is *spend-in* to transfer assets to marginalised communities and other initiatives for the purchase of land, buildings, and other required post capitalist infrastructure (e.g. bioregional regeneration and sovereignty). Related to this, foundations can blend grant dollars with endowment funds to be more fluid and flexible in the ways and types of organisations and projects they can support (e.g. funding groups and social movements that do not have not-for-profit status).

We also recommend the abolition of milestone reports and bureaucratic processes, including reimagining and redesigning the entire due-diligence process. We suggest moving towards *relationally-based giving practices* focused on generosity, reciprocity

---

[204] We recommend reading the important book *Hospicing Modernity* by Vanessa Machado de Oliveira. See Machado de Oliveira (2018).

and trust. This could include other democratic means of giving, such as giving circles and/or flow funding, where embedded activists are given set amounts of funds to distribute within their respective communities. Another obvious practice is to diversify the board and leadership to include more activists and practitioners who will challenge power, ontological biases, and institutional comfort.

Then comes the endowment work. We believe it is a necessary precondition that foundations begin divesting from equity markets and engage with the critical work of historical reparations. This will require a fundamental shift in the notion of organisational preservation, growth, legacy and other historical entitlements.

All of these practices require *onto-shifts* at their core: they are about letting go of the very idea of private ownership and decision-making, entitlements and privileges. These practices are not merely being made because they are the right thing to do, but because this wealth is the world's collective endowment; stewardship is a shared responsibility; and capital should be liberated in service to the living world.

REFLECTION PRACTICES:
DEEPENING WITH THE FIVE ELEMENT MANDALA

- PAUSE -

...

Here are a few further questions for you to write and contemplate so as to deepen your perspective with the *Five Elements mandala*:

- Map your current philanthropic giving within the *Five Elements mandala*. How does your personal strategy feed into your ontology and ability to create and contribute to the superstructure as mycelial service?

- What does the *Five Elements mandala* bring into focus for you, your organisation or movement, your way of considering philanthropy in these times?

- Where would your organisation embrace or resist some of the elements and ideas we have offered in this mandala?

- What onto-shifts are necessary to support transition pathways to life-centric systems?

ARTWORK ON FOLLOWING PAGE:
**"LLAMA DE LA TIERRA,
AGUITA DEL ALMA"**
~ ALIXA GARCÍA ~

EMBEDMENT WITHIN THE GAIAN ENTELECHY

~

"The sky gave me its heart
Because it knew mine was not large enough to care
For the Earth the way
It did."

- Rabia, 8th century Sufi mystic [205]

"Many worlds have gone before this one. Our traditional histories are tightly woven with the fabric of the birthing and ending of worlds. Through these cataclysms we have gained many lessons that have shaped who we are and how we are to be with one another. Our ways of being are informed through finding harmony through and from the destruction of worlds. The Elliptic. Birth. Death. Rebirth."

- Rethinking the Apocalypse: An Indigenous Anti-Futurist Manifesto [206]

One of the starkest omissions in the pyramid logic of neoliberal hegemony is the fact that it is not embedded within anything greater than itself. There is no Earthly home, no ecological womb from whence it came. It believes itself to be a free-standing agent, as if the ideology of political economy could be *sui generis*, a category unto itself.

In contrast, the outer edge of spiral logic is embedded in the planetary ecology itself, the living Gaian whole of which we are only one interdependent component. We use the term Gaia, from the Western tradition, both to acknowledge that Gaia is the Greek term for the Earth Mother herself, and as a nod to the scientific tradition, rooted in the study of Earth systems proposed by James Lovelock, Lynn Margulis and many others. The *Gaia Hypothesis* refers to the Earth as a living organism in which millions of constitutive species create a synergistic, complex, adaptive system that creates and maintains the conditions for thriving life on the planet.[207]

---

[205] Ladinsky (Ed.) (2002), p.9
[206] Indigenous Action (2020), p.5
[207] The idea of planet Earth as a living organism of many interrelated complex systems was

Of course, Indigenous peoples and other civilisations rooted in ecological and spiritual wisdom have understood this since the genesis of their cultures, and have therefore oriented their ways of living and being as such. In Latin America, the Incan goddess Pachamama is often invoked to refer to the Great Mother that creates and contains all of life.

As its own being, Pachamama or Gaia is understood as having an "entelechy". This is a Greek word that comes from a composite of *en* "within", *telos* "end" or "perfection" and *echein* "in a certain state". Thus, she contains her perfect end state within herself. She is whole, complete, vital, self-regulating, and interdependent. There can be no political-economic superstructure, neoliberal or otherwise, that is not an embedded subset of the greater Gaian whole, whether we acknowledge it or not. Our inability to understand and integrate this primary premise of reality is one of the key drivers of our current predicament.

Gaia herself is, of course, already embedded within an emergent, expanding universe that exhibits the same laws of physics as she does, including quantum and macro-phenomena, such as gravitational and electromagnetic wave fields, strong and weak forces, quantum nonlocality, relationality, relativity, and other universal factors.

We keep our gaze in relation to the Gaian entelechy, recognizing it is a fractal of the cosmic whole. Her bounds and constraints are illustrative of what is necessary for us to remember. As the quantum physicist Carlo Rovelli states: "I believe that in order to understand reality, we have to keep in mind that reality is this network of relations, of reciprocal information, that weaves the world."[208]

Any emerging post capitalist system – i.e. any mycelial superstructure – must be firmly rooted in the Earthplane whilst humbly acknowledging the agency of the Gaian whole. In *Down to Earth: Politics in the New Climatic Regime*, Bruno Latour suggests that humanity's common attractor could be described as "[the Terrestrial] with a capital T to emphasise that we are referring to a concept, and even specifying in advance where

---

reintroduced to scientific literature through the lens of atmospheric homeostasis by James Lovelock and Lynn Marguilis and has been provocative to the scientific community ever since. See Lovelock & Margulis (1974).

[208] Rovelli, (2014), p.254

we are headed: the Terrestrial as a *new political actor.*"[209] He goes on to say that the Terrestrial is "no longer the milieu or the background of human action…[it] is no longer the framework for human action… because it *participates* in that action."[210]

What is important here is that the Terrestrial, the living planet, is understood as having her own entelechy, and both human and Gaian reactions are discursive interplays of dialogue, gesture, ritual, and phenomenon amongst humans and the whole. "If the composition of the air we breathe depends on living beings, the atmosphere is no longer simply the environment in which living beings are located and in which they evolve; it is, in part, a result of their actions. In other words, there are not organisms on one side and an environment on the other, but a co-production by both. *Agencies are redistributed.*"[211]

This is a good starting place for our desired humility in our search for post capitalist realities. *Agencies are redistributed.* Of course, agency was never what we thought it was: for hundreds of years our notions of agency and will have been tainted by our hubris, exceptionalism, racialized supremacy, Cartesian separation of the human mind and nature, Newtonian metaphors of a machine-like universe and other limited beliefs. The agency of Gaia is negotiated amongst millions of other species' agencies, with forces that we are yet to understand, and the emergent, animate whole which, by definition, cannot have inanimate parts.

This is part of the *onto-shifts* we have been gesturing towards. How we see the world and our place in it determines how we understand and perceive the boundaries of 'legitimate' knowledge. This then affects our moral/ethical stance on how we interact with the world. These are not linear processes, but cyclical flows that feed each other in discursive, self-reflexive, interdependent ways. Hence we offer the move from pyramid logic to more spiralling ways of sensing, being and knowing.

This is also why we have grounded the *Five Elements mandala* in the *Earth* element when creating post capitalist infrastructure. The regeneration of land and soil are not simply rational strategies for sequestering carbon. Regeneration is a hymn, a restorative act, an offering for reconciliation, a rebalancing of right relationships, and a gesture towards the redemptive healing required as a result of human ignorance.

---

[209] Latour (2018) p.40
[210] Ibid p.42
[211] Ibid pp.75-76

We open the call and response channel that allows us to become apprentices of deep time and non-dualistic thought.

Latour suggests a strategy where: "We must make two complementary movements that modernization has made contradictory: *attaching oneself* to the soil on the one hand, *becoming attached to the world* on the other... Bringing together the two opposing figures of the soil and the world... The ground, the soil in this sense, cannot be appropriated. One belongs to it; it belongs to no one."[212]

Our interpretation of this is that our ability to attach ourselves to the soil has the potential to initiate us into the golden thread of reciprocity, where we never extract more than the whole is able and willing to give to us, never more than an ecosystem can regenerate. Our ability to attach ourselves to the world means that we may be initiated into life and death, learning how to love so deeply that we will ultimately know how to let go. This includes abandoning the techno-utopian fantasies of a Singularity event where Artificial Intelligence surpasses human knowledge or terraforming Mars or technological immortality through virtual reality. These are escapist measures that prevent us from the critical task of *coming down to Earth* and making a sanctuary here once again.

As we acknowledge and honour the agency, intentionality and self-consciousness of the living planet and all the species that make it whole, we too will be granted our own (co)agency in the cosmic unfolding. As we grant dignity to others, we too will be granted dignity. As we honour death, we will be granted deeper access to life. This is perhaps part of what it means to be in dialogue with an animistic planetary whole, with each of its species as kin. This requires more than a shift of gaze. It requires a practice of remembering so that we can gaze anew.

Reciprocity, mutual respect, care and consent are among the currencies of this remembering. Relationality is its fabric. Empathy is its texture. Harmony, equilibrium and balance could be its outcomes in the superposition of possibilities, rather than simply a collapse, or an Armageddon, or any other Judeo-Christian, Euro-American, millenarian fantasy of "the end". Of course, those options currently bear the weightiest probability under the orbit of our dominant culture.

---

[212] Latour (2018) p.92

In brief, contrary to linear logic, the manner of our approach may determine where we go.

If we approach the meta-crisis with humility, awareness, and a certain gratitude for being entrusted with what we have as individuals, as relations, as a species, perhaps the planet will respond with a different outcome than if we continue destroying, extracting, hoarding, consuming and ignoring the obvious consequences of our behaviour. If we are driven by the desire to deepen a collective field of care and belonging and in service to something greater, and more intimate, than ourselves, perhaps Gaia will unlock for us new-ancient-emerging pathways that we did not even know existed.

> *As we acknowledge and honour the agency, intentionality and self-consciousness of the living planet and all the species that make it whole, we too will be granted our own (co)agency in the cosmic unfolding. As we grant dignity to others, we too will be granted dignity. As we honour death, we will be granted deeper access to life. This is perhaps part of what it means to be in dialogue with an animistic planetary whole, with each of its species as kin. This requires more than a shift of gaze. It requires a practice of remembering so that we can gaze anew.*

This of course cannot be the main aim of embodying the *onto-shift*, because we would again be reifying the thought-form of commodification (another means-to-ends strategy). A question we must ponder is what archetypal roles do we want to play at the "end of history", in the midst of the so-called Anthropocene? Perhaps our answer to this question will determine what pathways are open to us now.

REFLECTION EXERCISE: ANCESTRAL CONTEMPLATION AND ANIMATE DIALOGUE

- PAUSE -

...

As we reflect on the journey thus far, we have asked you to consider spiral logic, to examine your deeper cosmology, consider the Five Elements mandala and imagine how this might apply to the work of creating post capitalist philanthropy. We now offer two final reflection exercises. The first situates us within our respective lineages: the legacies, traumas, biases, resources and endowments we have inherited. The second asks us to consider other ways in which we may be able to engage in dialogue with the animate world.

ARTWORK ON FOLLOWING PAGE:
"ANCIENT FUTURES"
~ FEDERICO CRUZ ~

PART I – Ancestral Contemplation

Perhaps this journey has revealed our personal biases, our historical interests, our familial origin stories, and perhaps even our ancestor's lifelines entangled with our preferences, desires, and proclivities towards some issues or inquiries over others. The word 'ancestors' often invokes a range of responses, from bafflement to over-specificity. In order to facilitate this exercise, we offer multiple cosmologies as entry-points.

Here are five lenses which you can use to answer the questions below:

1. Within some First Nations' cosmologies in Turtle Island, the symbol of the Totem can be defined as "that which nourished your ancestors." The Totem represents the ancestors that fed and sustained our ancestors.
2. From an emerging scientific view, there has been an evolution in understanding about what is known as junk DNA. It is now being understood that junk DNA contains an electromagnetic charge (similar to our organs)[213]. One could argue that this resonant field is a means by which our ancestral lines communicate with us. Empirically, we see this work emerging in the field of epigenetics that demonstrates how we hold the ancestral memories (traumas, etc.) of at least five to seven generations.
3. From the perspective of mystical traditions that believe in reincarnation, we may also be able to communicate with ancestors from past lives, and/or our past lives can be seen as our ancestors.
4. From an archetypal perspective, you can consider what ancestral archetypes you embody and what these archetypal roles may have taught you before you first performed them. Some of the standard archetypal roles in Jungian theory include the queen/king, mother/father, priest/priestess, warrior, artist, magician, explorer, lover, caregiver, jester, rebel and sage.
5. In Ancient Egyptian cosmology, there is the notion of Star Nation ancestors, in which a complex of cosmic souls chooses a physical DNA line in which to incarnate. This is another lens which you can bring to the inquiry below.

---

[213] Buehler (1 September 2021)

We are not suggesting that any of these conceptions are "true", rather, that you can use them as lenses or entry points into feeling, thinking and sensing your ancestral lines. We ask that you spend some time journaling your first responses to the questions below. Try to put yourself in a quiet place with no disturbances. The questions are simply prompts. Please write in free-flow form (or draw), follow your intuition, and then reflect after you've read and responded to all the prompts.

1. Trace the migratory path of your physical ancestors. As you are doing this, honour the physical lands they may have walked upon. Draw maps if that's helpful.
2. What burdens, traumas, existential threats did your ancestors confront? What haunted them?
3. What nourished them, what gave them sustenance, what brought them joy?
4. What unresolved work, issues, thoughtforms may still be lingering in the ancestral realms of your lineage?
5. What healing or redemption work wants to happen through you?
6. Why do you think you incarnated into your specific line (DNA, archetypal, other)? Even if you don't believe you had a choice, we ask that you temporarily exercise a "willing suspension of disbelief" to answer the question.
7. If you knew you would be the last person in your lineage, would this change your behaviour? If so, in what ways?
8. What type of ancestor are you becoming?

...

PART II – Animate Dialogue

Here are some questions to deepen your dialogic practice:

1. Write down the various ways in which you currently practise being in dialogue with the living planet?
2. What do you believe Gaia wants? What are her desires? What is the role of human beings within the Gaian whole?
3. What archetypal roles are you playing within the Gaian whole?
4. Go for a walk and notice if there is a tree, a plant, an animal, or insect you are particularly drawn to. How could and do you communicate with this being? What might this being have to say to you?
5. **Create an altar**: a physical ritual space for meditation, contemplation, and/or prayer. You can use a small table or corner of a room. You can include symbolic items to represent the four elements (e.g. a stone to represent *Earth*, a feather to represent *Air*, etc.); include an object that represents the fifth element of *Ether*, of the healing of life-force. Ask the emergent cosmos what it wants to be and what role you could play in humbly stewarding a vision for the future. Check in with your altar at least once a day in the morning (and ideally once in the evening before sleep) for a period of 7-10 days, or ideally, a one month cycle from new moon to new moon or full moon to full moon.

WALKING INTO THE UNKNOWN

ARTWORK ON FOLLOWING PAGE:
"THE THREE CARRIERS OF THE WORLD:
YOU, THE PLANET, YOUR COMMUNITY"
~ FEDERICO CRUZ ~

PART FOUR

WALKING INTO THE UNKNOWN

~

"Be patient toward all that is unsolved in your heart and try to love the questions themselves, like locked rooms and like books that are now written in a very foreign tongue. Do not now seek the answers, which cannot be given to you because you would not be able to live them. And the point is, to live everything. Live the questions now. Perhaps you will then gradually, without noticing it, live along some distant day into the answer."

- Rainer Maria Rilke [214]

"To travel without a map, to travel without a way. They did, long ago That misdirection became the way. After the Door of No Return, a map was only a set of impossibilities, a set of changing locations."

- Dionne Brand [215]

We have been on a journey that started from the pyramid logic of neoliberalism, and its driving forces of colonialism, patriarchy, enslavement, hierarchy, genocide, violence and consumption to engage a spiral logic that asks us to reflect on and take radical responsibility for our belief systems and inner structures in order to (re)form relational webs that build social ecologies, which then build biomes, feeding into post capitalist mycelial superstructures nested within the Gaian entelechy.

We have gestured towards the nature of the spiral, which is, among other things, interdependent, fractal, multi-directional, self-reflexive, discursive, non-linear and non-dualistic. We are not trying to engage in a process of creating emergence, but, rather, attempting to create conditions that allow us to intra-act with emergence in a more contextually-sensitive manner. Rather than dualistic binaries we are attempting to enter, or more accurately, re-enter the continuum of Life. This requires

---

[214] Rilke (1994), p.31
[215] Brand (2002), p.262

an understanding, a renewed relationship, and a renegotiation with life-force itself.

Truth (with a capital T) and capitalism are fundamentally incompatible. In a world where anything can be bought and sold, the first casualty is our integrity. The second casualty, as a direct result of the first, is the loss of life-force. When one cannot protect the integrity of their own life-force, one cannot commune with, let alone, defend the sanctity of Life.

Our individual and collective life-force is directly affected by the structures and systems in which we are enmeshed. Hence, we cannot simply shift our internal landscapes without also creating commensurate shifts in the material, physical structures that play a constitutive role in the formation of our realities (i.e. moving from capitalism to post capitalisms). Similarly, we cannot re-imagine systems and institutions of oppression without commensurate *onto-shifts*. Both of these processes, the so-called inner and the outer worlds, mirror each other in a very similar manner to spiral logic (i.e. interdependently, fractally, reflexively, discursively, non-linearly and non-dualistically).

Due to the limitations of the written word and the flat dimension of screens and books, it is not fully clear that the spiral moves upwards towards emergence. In essence, it contains its own entelechy, embedded within the Gaian whole. Some may say that this direction is towards ever-greater complexity, while others may claim that it moves towards entropy.

The question we now sit with as we bring this text to a close is how we can bring to life the myriad of practices that activate the upward direction of the spiral in service to life-force and magnify the feedback loops towards the thriving of living systems?

What came to us was a circular magnet sitting upon the spiral with three words: surrender, traverse, (re)enter. Just as there is a magnetic circle of desired pathways sitting at the base of the Five Elements mandala – in *Restoration & Solidarity, Transformation & Creation,* and the *(Re)cultivation of Life-Force* – there is a trinity of practices, ways of being, sitting upon or within the spiral logic. Surrender, traverse, (re)enter. These are our strange attractors.

SURRENDER, TRAVERSE, (RE)ENTER

SURRENDER CONTROL
TRAVERSE THE THRESHOLD
(RE)ENTER THE CONTINUUM

Surrender is about letting go of control, the great addiction of capitalist modernity. Control manifests in a myriad of ways, from the need for certainty to the perpetuation of scarcity logic. Surrender is related to shedding the Cartesian anxiety[216], Newtonian certainty, Euclidian fixity, modernity's fixation on problem/solution, and other coordinates of the colonised mind and body.

Within neoliberalism, control is often represented through money. In an ontology where everything can be perceived as a commodity, money becomes a primary avenue to certainty. Of course, some degree of control might be necessary, or even desirable, especially when trying to keep body and soul together. But the hoarding of vast amounts of wealth at the expense of other beings' right to exist, and the destruction of our ecosystem is a perverse form of control.

The direction and strict management of a small fraction of wealth under the guise of philanthropy is an extension of this control. Although we have highlighted some of the means by which to let go of control (for example through community-led foundations, communal land-trusts & stewardship of land models, cascading commons, spend-in and other mechanisms), in the end these are decisions that one

---

[216] Richard J. Bernstein first used the term 'Cartesian Anxiety' to refer to the desire and expectation of unchangeable ontological certainty. See Bernstein (1983), p.66.

must make amongst the myriad of relational entanglements, within the constraints of their perceived and negotiated agency. Surrender is an on-going practice, to be deepened with willingness and humility.

> *Truth (with a capital T) and capitalism are fundamentally incompatible. In a world where anything can be bought and sold, the first casualty is our integrity. The second casualty, as a direct result of the first, is the loss of life-force. When one cannot protect the integrity of their own life-force, one cannot commune with, let alone, defend the sanctity of Life.*

We use 'traverse' in the sense of travelling across or through a terrain. Crossing a threshold comes to mind. Through surrender, we enter the gateway to a liminal space that we must then cross, perhaps perpetually. This can trigger ambiguity or disorientation. Crossing the threshold may require the creation of new-ancient-emerging behaviours and ways of sensing/knowing/being. One may characterise this accompanying shift as a move from an *ontology of separation* to a *relational ontology*. One may be so bold as to describe these as *liberation ontologies*. The aim of these perspectives is the liberation of all beings and the thriving of the living, sacred world and cosmos, acknowledging that how we see the world is a radical, political-spiritual praxis that informs how we take part in its co-creation.

Traversing is the realm of state-change in the alchemical sense. As we shed both thought-forms and the burdened weight of accumulation, we create a space and lightness that allows us to cross thresholds, to create spiritual and neural pathways that can help reinforce the emerging patterns, to anchor us within *liberation ontologies*. Addressing, integrating or even surrendering to the meta-crisis may be a civilizational initiation, but it also requires us as individuals and communities to traverse thresholds of various kinds.

The crossing of these chasms leads to a continuum, a stream of multiple realities and varied types of consciousness, beyond the binaries of past versus future, old versus new, mind versus body, transcendent versus immanent, nature versus culture, inner versus outer. It is an enchanted continuum of remembering that links us to our ancestral pasts and to possible, adjacent futures rooted in a symbiosis with the animate universe. It is a continuum of deep time that is eternally affected by our role as participants in the deep present. To return full circle to *The Ancient Egyptian Book of the Dead,* Osiris says: "Time reaches in both directions, knotted in the golden orb of the moment. The eye opens, the heart opens, the navel yawns and takes the world in its belly. Beneath him the snake feels the movement of Earth. Everything else is sky. This moment is eternity."[217]

We are dealing here with the paradox of time. As we have invoked throughout this text, there is a small window of linear time in which capital can be usefully employed to create post capitalist realities and support the necessary work of *restoration & solidarity, transformation & creation* and the *(re)cultivation of life-force.*

In addition to the urgency of *chronos* time, Occidental clock time, there is *kairos* time: time as cyclical, co-existing, ever-present, interpenetrating, inviting. As we intra-act with the unfolding *chronos*, we also mutually implicate the manifestations and entry-points into *kairos*. There is no tidy distinction between past, present and future; we are in a state of embryonic unfolding. Our awareness and self-reflexivity induces karmic waves on the ocean of eternity.

As we deepen our embodiment of values such as humility, generosity, interdependence, reciprocity, solidarity, and interbeing, the Gaian entelechy and the fractal cosmos mirror back to us superpositions of possibility. As Karen Barad reminds us, "Meeting each moment being alive to the possibilities of becoming, is an ethical call, an invitation that is written into the very matter of being and becoming."[218] As we expand the mytho-poetic landscape and the corresponding creation of embodied knowledge and cultures, we may avail ourselves to the direct wisdom of the Gaian entelechy and the quiet whispers of that which is beyond our perception.

---

[217] Ellis (1988), p.170
[218] Barad (2014), p.396

REFLECTION EXERCISE:
CREATING POST CAPITALIST VOWS

...

The root causes of our meta-crisis are interconnected.
I vow to understand them.

The delusions of capitalist modernity are inexhaustible.
I vow to transmute and transform them.

The alternatives are boundless.
I vow to perceive, create and amplify them.

Post capitalist realities are inevitable, yet delicate.
I vow to practise, nurture and embody them.

...

Consider what it means to make and take vows. We have taken inspiration from a version of the Buddhist Bodhisattva vows[219] – to create post capitalist vows as part of our journey through surrender, traverse, and (re)enter.

What would your rendition of post capitalist vows look like?
Write them down and share them with a trusted ally.

ARTWORK ON FOLLOWING PAGE:
"THE SURRENDERER"
~ ALIXA GARCÍA ~

---

[219] Adapted from the Four Great Bodhisattva Vows. See Upaya Institute (June 1, 2017).

As we examine the consequences of wealth extraction and accumulation, with its corollary of philanthropy, and the unattended spiritual implications, vistas of reciprocity and generosity may open to us. As we start to witness the inner/outer mirroring of the meta-crisis, we may transform our understanding of agency, duality and linearity to be more deeply and responsibly embedded in the animistic whole which affects us and is affected by us. As we embrace paradox and abandon the addiction of certainty, entitlement and control, we may see that alternatives outside of the false binaries offered by capitalist modernity have always been with us. As we take seriously the fierce urgency of now, we may access a continuum of time that opens possibilities of radical restoration and transformation.

The harbinger of post capitalist realities may be as simple as laying one's forehead upon the naked Earth in contemplation of the liberation of all beings. It may also require discarding the weight and burden of accumulated wealth (perhaps recasting it as a ticking time-bomb of suffering, as one interviewee described it) while holding that same liberatory intention. How far we go as a civilisation may depend on how far each of us are willing to go, how much each of us is willing to open and surrender, as entangled knots in a greater tapestry.

Imagine we created a reality where we only engaged in activities that create conditions for the emergence of beauty, life-force and enchantment? What if we created a context in which the will and entelechy of all beings could manifest with full sovereignty? What would a world look like where we envisioned the consequences of our actions two-hundred or five-hundred or even a thousand years into the future and only then created our contribution to our descendants' societies, as if we were them?

Rather than vocations or purpose, what would happen if we asked the living world how to best use our life-force in service to its desired unfolding? What if we discarded commodified clock-time with its assigned dollar value? What if we could create a world where our ancestors could fulfil themselves through us? What would happen if we structured our political-economic-cultural superstructures so that all human beings could pursue activities that brought them joy in service to the collective whole?

What if philanthropy could render itself obsolete in one or two generations, hospicing itself in service to post capitalist realities worth living? What if we could start again, not like escapists seeking novel beginnings, but as participants in a cyclical continuum of initiation?

> *As we examine the consequences of wealth extraction and accumulation, with its corollary of philanthropy, and the unattended spiritual implications, vistas of reciprocity and generosity may open to us. As we start to witness the inner/outer mirroring of the meta-crisis, we may transform our understanding of agency, duality and linearity to be more deeply and responsibly embedded in the animistic whole which affects us and is affected by us.*

We do not ask these questions in the hope of final answers, but as invitations to stay with the trouble, to recast questions as doorways to other realities.[220] Perhaps by asking these questions, and starting our inquiry, Gaia will notice. Perhaps she will meet us halfway. Perhaps more practice is in order.

Surrender control, traverse the threshold, and (re)enter the continuum of Life.

---

[220] "Questions are doorways to other realities" is a phrase used by Orland Bishop in a personal interview with the authors, December 1, 2021.

MYTHO-POETIC EPILOGUE

~

As we invoke surrender, traverse and (re)enter, it seems fitting and proper that we close this text with a final sojourn into the realm of the mytho-poetic. Similar to how we began with the myth of Osiris, the Ancient Egyptian god of justice, we now turn to his Sumerian counterpart: Inanna the goddess of love, war, fertility, sex, justice and power. In the epic poem, *The Descent of Inanna* (originating in ancient Mesopotamia circa 3500 BCE), our heroine journeys into the underworld, faces the consequences of her actions, confronts death and destruction by the hand of her sibling, and is resurrected with the assistance of other gods.[221]

Inanna, the Queen of Heaven and Earth, leaves her realm in the sky, to Earth, and then journeys down into the underworld to visit her recently widowed sister Ereshkigal, Queen of the Dead. Unlike the Duat of Ancient Egypt, the Sumerian underworld of Kur was conceived of as a dark, dreary cavern located deep underground; life there was envisioned as "a shadowy version of life on earth".[222]

The poem begins with the lines:

> *From the Great Above she opened her ear to the Great Below*
> *From the Great Above the goddess opened her ear to the Great Below*
> *From the Great Above Inanna opened her ear to the Great Below.* [223]

In the Sumerian language, the word for "ear" also means wisdom. Inanna is called to listen to the Great Below, the realm of dream, death, grief, depression, and the unconscious, because she seeks wisdom – something that can only come from beyond the culture and realms of Heaven and Earth, a wisdom beyond what she already has dominion over.[224] Without knowledge of loss, vulnerability, death, and mortality, she is not whole.

---

[221] Kramer (1963)
[222] Choksi (2014)
[223] Wolkstein & Kramer (1983), p.52
[224] Choksi (2014)

Upon her arrival at the gates of the underworld, Inanna knocks loudly and demands entrance: "I am Inanna, Queen of Heaven!" The gate-keeper asks why she wants entrance to the land "from which no traveller returns." Inanna has come to the underworld armed with the seven divine powers, including beautiful garments and jewels. Her sister, Ereshkigal, Queen of the Dead, is not pleased about her sister's arrival.

Ereshkigal commands each of the seven gates of the underworld to be bolted against Inanna. As Innana is let through, one gate at a time, she is required to remove one of her royal garments at each pass. As Inanna is stripped of her crown, beads, ring, sceptre, even her clothing, she is divested of her powers and her beauty. She enters the underworld naked, humble, and vulnerable.

In reverse fashion to the seven gates of initiation that Osiris traverses through, Inanna enters the throne room of Ereshkigal "naked and bowed low" and begins walking toward the throne when:

> *The Annuna, the judges of the Underworld, surrounded her*
> *They passed judgement against her.*
> *Then Ereshkigal fastened on Inanna the eye of death*
> *She spoke against her the word of wrath*
> *She uttered against her the cry of guilt*
> *She struck her.*
> *Inanna was turned into a corpse*
> *A piece of rotting meat*
> *And was hung from a hook on the wall.*[225]

---

[225] Wolkstein & Kramer (1983), p.60

Before going to the underworld, Inanna leaves instructions for help – a possible way back. After three days and three nights waiting, her mistress follows her commands and goes to Enki, Inanna's father-god for help. He creates two queer, non-binary beings called *galla* (sometimes referred to as "demons") that carry the water of life and seeds of Earth to aid Inanna in her ascent back to Earth.

The poem describes that while Inanna is rotting on the meat hook, her sister is in the pains of labour, pregnant with her dead husband's child. The *galla* sympathise with Ereshkigal and she, in gratitude, offers them whatever gift they ask for. The *galla* ask for Inanna's corpse, and Ereshkigal grants their wish. They then revive Inanna with the seeds and the waters of Life. By this gift, she rises from the dead. Simultaneously, Ereshkigal, the Queen of Death, gives birth, thus solidifying her position as the harbinger of transformation.

Inanna returns initiated as the Queen of Death, Heaven, and Earth. She returns with knowledge and wisdom of all three realms, including the depth of death, destruction, consequence, transformation, and life in its fullness. Here we find one of the keys to many ancient myths: the assertion that death and birth are the same source.

As the Jungian scholar Betty De Shong Meador states: "The myth carries a double message. One is that the accomplishments of civilization based on the masculine imagination [...] focused on achievement, *and* that focus separates its citizens from an ongoing awareness of primordial nature ruled by a female, a goddess, Ereshkigal. Inanna, who has so successfully adapted to Sumerian civilization, ruling from her position of queen of the upper world, has lost her connection to the vast feminine world of natural processes, natural cycles..."[226]

Inanna sensed she was missing an aspect of her being. She listened, she went against the orders of the other gods, she went in search of a deeper wisdom. To find it, she had to relinquish her powers, encounter death and decay, and with the assistance of powers beyond her own, she was resurrected.

By bringing back the power of Ereshkigal, the myth instructs us to move beyond our anthropocentric ways of seeing and living (Inanna's limited reign over Heaven and Earth). The Goddess of Death cuts through comfort, manipulation and self-serving

---
[226] Meador (1992), p.33

superficiality. She shows us that humans and our civilizations are not supreme. It is the dual knowledge of the mysteries of the underworld and the initiate's path through death that are what allow Inanna to re-enter the continuum of both Life and Death.

The myth of Inanna teaches us how we may learn to surrender, even in the midst of self-annihilation and civilisational collapse. Our attachments must be dissolved. We must be willing to go into the underworld, to be hung on the proverbial meat hook, and to offer our crowns of certainty, our treasures of control, our robes of vanity, and the desires we feel entitled to enact. In so doing, we may be purified and composted, like the rotting leaves on the forest floor; we may be given the creativity of life anew.

In this sense, Inanna's story points to our current trajectory within the meta-crisis. We are in the midst of what we might call the *Age of Consequence*. Five thousand years of pillage, destruction, hierarchy, patriarchy, racism, violence and war have led to our journey into the underworld. We are being thrown down into an initiatory descent.

We may find our way. And we may not.

Let us walk each other into the unknown as we surrender control, traverse thresholds, and re-enter the continuum of Life and Death.

~ CLOSING PRAYER ~
/ ACKNOWLEDGEMENTS /

Our plant teachers and allies that guided this text; the Vine of the Ancestors, Chacruna, Mapacho, Huachuma, Marosa, Bobinsana, Piñon Blanco, Rosa, Noyarao, Chiric Sanango, and the Niños … The gods and prophets that sustained our cultures, beliefs, souls and visions. The animals, plants, fruits, vegetables that nourished both us and our ancestors, and are therefore, our beloved researcher whose fingerprints are found throughout this book. The TRC team; Ashima Bhardwaj, who leads TRC's operations in coca, and Adrian Oosthuizen, our beloved researcher with keen aesthetics and being. May peace be upon you. Vittoria Cardona for her creative direction in coca and book design, keen aesthetics and being. May peace be upon you. And of course the late Gustavo Esteva, who embodied post-capitalist thought and helped shape these ideas through our gatherings 2017, 2019 and 2022. Our TRC allies that deepened our inquiries and generously nurtured book experiments; Our beloved allies at the Defend the Sacred Alliance. And the NoVo Foundation that generously nurtured book experiments (US and New Zealand) for their support and trust during the early years of TRC. The Rumi Foundation (UK) and the Namaste Foundation. Martin Winiecki, Mehul Sangham, Matthew Monahan, Brian Berkopec, Ashish Kothari, Hickel, Carlin Quinn, Pat McCabe, Sarah Buie, Barry Knight, Sean Thackurdeen, Farhad Ibhrahmi, Jeronimo Calderon, Tim Wynnne-McCarthy, Julian Corner, Marai Larasi, Carne Ross, Sohroh Nabatian, Sonali Balajee, Jennifer Buffett, and all of our other interviewees. Nnimmo Bassy, and constraints of the written word.

Divine Emergence (Ya' Allah). The Great Mother, the Gaian entelechy, the Earth beneath our feet; the water that sustains us; the air that we breathe; the fire that moves us; the ether that binds us together.

Our ancestors, those who came before us in order for us to be here now. May we be your living prayers.

Our family, chosen and otherwise. Our lovers, past, present and future for the gift of co-hosting the deity of Eros. Tierra Valiente for holding us in all the ways she does.

Our artist/designer siblings: Federico Cruz, Alixa Garcia, and the South African contingent from OCTOPI, Leila Kidson and Cara Eyre.

Our Accompaniment Circle: Orland Bishop, Andrea Panaritis, Kumi Naidoo, Peter Lipman, Tiokasin Ghosthorse, Bayo Akomolafe, Blessol Gathoni, and Preeta Bansal.

The Christopher Reynolds Foundation and its brave board, especially our dear compañera Andrea Panaritis, for inspiration and trusting towards post capitalist philanthropy.

Our siblings at Culture Hack Labs and its older sister, The Rules collective. And our community at Brave Earth, especially Maxine Shifrin, Filipa Cardoso and Yael Maranza.

The New World Foundation – Colin Greer, for the ongoing wisdom, counsel and support in harbouring the TRC.

Our ally Daraja Press, especially the indomitable Firoz Manji for his support and counsel in publishing this book.

Our beloved allies and friends, who gifted us time for conversations, discourse and debate: Martin Kirk, Jason, Nate Hagens, Asher Miller, Pia Infante, David Bollier, Tom Kruze, Anastiya Sengupt, Taj James, Felipe Viveros, Aubrey Yee, Gopal Dayaneni, Scott Fitzmorris, Sofia Arroyo, Ron Regan, Helga Rainer, Nwamaka Agbo, Louisa Zondo, Justine Epstein, Tomas Bjorkman, Jules Peck, Manish Jain.

Gratitude to the English language for reaching us limitations.

Shukran Lillah, Wal Hamdulillah.

APPENDIX A: GLOSSARY

~

Age of Consequence: Our current moment in civilisational history where five thousand years of pillage, destruction, hierarchy, patriarchy, racism, violence and war have culminated in our descent into the meta-crisis.

Ancient Futures: This term is borrowed from Helena Norberg-Hodge's book of the same name. We have altered her initial meaning (which was specific to the community of Ladakh, India) to indicate a merger between past, present and future as acts of creation/remembering of ancient knowledge, culture and ways of knowing, sensing and being as necessary for inclusion into a meaningful response to the problems of capitalist modernity.

Animism: A descriptive umbrella term for worldviews that consider the world – and therefore its constituent parts – as alive, interdependent and relational. This includes but is not limited to panpsychism, some forms of idealism and many pre-Cartesian notions of a living universe in which non-humans and even objects can have agency, entelechy and souls.

Anthropocene: A proposed name for the current geological epoch, with most significant impact on ecological systems (including climate change) being made by human activity. Though still unofficial, the most common suggestion is that the anthropocene began in the 1950s.

Capitalist modernity: Capitalist modernity is a term borrowed from Abdullah Öcalan's *Manifesto for a Democratic Civilization: The Age of Masked Gods and Disguised Kings*. We use the term interchangeably with neoliberalism, late-stage capitalism and other descriptors of our current paradigm. The advantage of this term is that it refers to both the political economy and the deeper cultural project of colonialism, imperialism, positivism, rationalism and materialism, i.e. the project of a totalising modernity based on separation from the living world.

Cartesian anxiety: Refers to the anxiety born out of the desire and expectation for unchangeable ontological certainty that has been cultivated in Western civilisation since the Enlightenment, specifically referring to the introduction of Descartes' mind-body dualism. The term speaks to the desire for unshakeable truth to be obtainable through objective, scientific reasoning. It was first coined by Richard J. Bernstein in his 1983 book *Beyond Objectivism and Relativism: Science, Hermeneutics, and Praxis*.

Cascading commons: A strategy to achieve larger spend-downs while fulfilling existing grantmaking commitments. One foundation agrees to spend down its endowment, another foundation, with the capacity for more grant-making, would agree to cover the difference in grants that would result from the reduced endowment for the period of the initial foundation's spend-down.

Complex Adaptive Systems: Systems whose outputs are greater than the sum of their parts and unpredictable due to dynamic interactions between the system and its context as well as between its constituent parts. Once a network becomes sufficiently complex, it becomes self-organising and self-preserving.

Degrowth: Refers to the social, political and economic movement that critiques the foundational premise that economic growth is the most important imperative for global and national economies. The movement de-emphasises economic growth for social considerations and is sensitive to North-South relationships and the fact that many economies that have undergone historic exploitation now require growth, while calling for industrial nations to de-grow their economies while addressing inequities and ecological overshoot.

Distributed fascism: Refers to the "necessary exploitation" of humans and more-than-human realms by individuals within the dominant capitalist framework because of the structural requirement of perpetual growth. Although most individuals do not have an intention to exploit or exhibit fascist tendencies, the cultural context of "survival of the fittest", the "invisible hand" and other norms creates a distributed violence in society and upon the natural world.

Embodied cognition: An umbrella term for approaches to cognition that are rooted in the body and somatic expression. Here, cognition is informed by the body and the physical environment; it is not simply limited to the brain or conceptual frames of the thinking mind.

Enclosure: A term for privatised land ownership, that refers to the appropriation of "common land" thereby depriving commoners of their ancient right to access the bounty of the natural world within the bounds of reciprocity.

Entanglement: In quantum physics, particles whose quantum state cannot be explained independently from the states of the other particles are entangled. We use the word entanglement to refer to the complex set of relationships all beings and things have to one another, including humans, non-humans and the living world.

Epistemology: A branch of philosophy and common term used to refer to inquiries which deal with the production of knowledge. It covers questions such as: How do we come to know things? How do we know what we think we know? What different kinds of knowledge exist? Whose knowledge is considered more valuable and why?

Ethico-onto-epistemology: Karen Barad's term refers to the nexus of ethics, epistemology and ontological points of view. The concept suggests that what we perceive in the world (ontology), what we believe about these perceptions (epistemology), and how we choose to navigate in the world are not separate, but emerge materially in an ongoing dynamic that co-determines our ethical stance. That is, the nature of reality, the nature of knowledge, and the nature of ethics are entangled, not fixed, final or determinate.

Fugitive epistemologies: Nigerian poet and author Bayo Akomolafe uses this term to refer to other ways of knowing and being that originate or are popular in the margins, cracks and borderlands. He suggests that we should centre these epistemologies in order to avoid "deploying the settler epistemologies that contributed to the geo-ecological hostilities of the present"[227]. He defines fugitivity as rejecting the promise or hope that the current paradigm can help or heal itself.

---

[227] Akomolafe (March 11, 2020)

Historical capitalism: Initially coined by sociologist Immanuel Wallerstein in his book of the same title. It refers to the historical societal choice to prioritise capital over all other alternative objectives.

Intra-action: Karen Barad uses the term intra-action (as opposed to interaction) to illustrate how entanglement precedes thingness. In other words, there are not simply "objective things" that make up the world and interact, but rather, relational lines. She suggests that ongoing relational dynamics are responsible for how things emerge.

Justice Plus Onto-Shifts: This concept refers to justice-as-becoming through pluralistic, liberatory, uniting and symbiotic approaches, rather than an idealised end-state of a justice we can know.

Kali Yuga: In the Vedic tradition of India, the Kali Yuga is the fourth and final yuga (world age) in the greater Yuga Cycle. It is preceded by the Treta Yuga (Silver Age), then the Dvapara Yuga (Bronze Age) and followed by the next cycle of Satya Yuga (Golden Age). It is widely considered that we are currently within the Kali Yuga. This notion of the "dark ages" is reflected in other cosmologies including the Hopi prophecy of the Sixth Sun; the Iroquois Seventh Fire; the Age of Degeneration in Buddhism; and the Time of the Underworld in Alchemical thought.

Late-stage capitalism: The current and final stage of capitalism where the requisite growth-imperative becomes highly unsustainable and untenable due to market saturation and the physical limits of extraction. This phase is the logical outcome of previous stages of proto-capitalism and industrial capitalism. It is characterised by extreme wealth concentration, a profusion of corporate monopolies & oligopolies, a rise in authoritarianism & state violence, ecological collapse and social breakdown.

Liberation ontology: New-ancient-emerging worldviews based on sensing/knowing/being with constitutive parts of the animistic universe as relational, interdependent, co-arising phenomena. The aim of these perspectives is the liberation of all beings and the thriving of the living world and cosmos, acknowledging that how we see the world is a radical, political-spiritual praxis that informs how we take part in its co-creation. This is contrasted with the more static, dominant worldview of capitalist modernity which can be characterised as a *separation ontology*. We have also used this term as an homage to *liberation theology*, the radical Catholic spiritual-political movement from the 1960s, largely driven by Latin American practitioners.

Meta-crisis: The meta-crisis refers to multiple co-arising and interconnected crises of social, ecological and political dimensions on a global scale. The crisis itself is a complex feedback of systems exacerbating one another. Also referred to as the polycrisis, we use meta-crises to name explicitly the ideological and ontological dimension that weaves together the causes and actions of crises.

New-ancient-emerging futures: Signifies the synthesis of the temporal trinity of past, present and future as non-linear phenomena where there are no tidy delineations between the three 'states'. We use *new* as the prefix in order to uproot the dominant cultural notion that *new* is most desirable; rather, we suggest that what is *new* is also the most immature, requiring both an ancient, historical lens and an emergent becoming that we do not yet know.

Non-dualistic thinking and embodiment: Holding two or more simultaneous and seemingly conflicting thoughts outside of dualistic, binary parameters of either/or. This concept includes both mental and somatic cognition as an aspirational approach to metabolising, integrating and working with new-ancient-emerging epistemologies, ontologies and cosmologies.

On-going colonial present: A term borrowed from geologist Katherin Yusoff's formidable text, *A Billion Black Anthropocenes or None*, indicating the on-going benefits that accrue to capital-holders and colonial settlers through the structural arrangements of capitalist modernity.

Omni-centricity: A scientific term borrowed from David Bohm referring to the locality of the centre of the universe residing everywhere throughout the universe.

Ontology: Ontology is about the nature of being and existence – the "isness" of something – of God, individual subjects, objects and reality. It is primarily about the identification, classification and disambiguation of "reality" itself. Ontology influences epistemology in that it frames the boundaries of what it means for something to exist, affecting notions of truth and sense-making in a discursive, reflexive manner.

Other ways of knowing, sensing and being: An umbrella concept for different modes of perception outside the dominant Occidental, linear, analytical logic-determined worldview. It includes logic as one avenue for making sense of the world that can be as important as other means. Rather than implying illogical alternatives to logic, the emphasis is on perceiving and experiencing complexity to inform understanding of lived experience and action as emergent phenomena.

Onto-shifts: Shifts in ontology that correlate with consequential shifts in epistemological and ethical points-of-view.

Overshoot: Taken from William Catton's sober ecological assessment of our narratives around technological progress and population growth. Overshoot refers to a species growing beyond an area's carrying capacity, resulting in either a drawdown of resources required for future populations; a die-off of the population whose growth has been an overshoot. Or in the case of humans in the current context, the die-off of other species within the ecology.

Praxis: An ongoing process by which theory is enacted, embodied, and realised.

Post anthropocentrism: Refers to a point-of-view that does not hold humankind as the exclusive locus or centre for decision making and consideration in design of and interaction with living systems.

Post capitalism: Post capitalism is a conceptual container of pluralities based on *shared values* that stem from an experience of the shortcomings of the existing system and the lived experience of capitalist alternatives. Some of the core uniting values include: reciprocity, altruism, cooperation, gratitude, gifting, regeneration, equity consciousness, communalism, shared governance & decision making, empathy, non-violence, interbeing and solidarity with all Life. We do not include a dash between post and capitalism to make clear that it is not simply a temporal state that exists *after* capitalism. Although the prefix post can imply a "context after" it also implies a state which is informed by the context prior to it.

Post capitalist futures: This concept acknowledges both future and existing post capitalist realities and the desire for a cultural context that cultivates more experiments & support of existing/nascent experimentation. These lived possibilities are here now, some have always been here, there will be more, their challenge to the dominant system is in some ways inevitable, and these realities do not require any future end-state to be validated.

Post capitalist infrastructure: Refers to infrastructure across cultures, relationality, pedagogy, health and wellbeing, as well as the myriad approaches to bioregional infrastructure that are required for the creation/amplification of post capitalist paradigms.

Post capitalist philanthropy: Given that philanthropy is an externality of capitalism itself, post capitalist philanthropy focuses on using capital to build post capitalist infrastructure in the short window of time that capitalist modernity continues to exist. It includes the eventual dissolution of philanthropy as part of a broader strategy of transition pathways. The invocation of post capitalist philanthropy invites a host of questions, including: How could philanthropy help transform capitalism when it was created by the very contradictions and inequities stemming from the system? Would any desirable post capitalist future still include the idea of a sector called philanthropy? How does philanthropy responsibly hospice itself in service to post capitalist futures?

Quantum ethics: An approach to applied ethics based on both an understanding of one's informing epistemologies, ontologies and cosmologies, in addition to a sense of uncertainty, indeterminacy and inability to fully know the most just course of action. Rather than categorical imperatives or golden rules, quantum ethics is based on moral humility, contextual-sensitivity, entanglement and non-duality (we are simultaneously subject and object, and perhaps, neither).

Somatic biographies: We use this term to refer to the historical locality of embodied ideas and thought forms within one's physical body.

Staying with the trouble: The titular phrase of Donna Harraway's seminal book refers to deliberate engagement with the crises of our time particularly through making kin with one another and the natural world in peculiar and unexpected collaborations. The focus is on surrender and being with the messiness of a problem rather than trying to "solve" them.

Spiritual-political praxis: Refers to the intersection of our inner landscapes and the material conditions we face in the world as co-constitutive mirrorings of each other.

Syntropic frames: The opposite of entropic frames (breakdown and degradation). Syntropic frames build more cohesion, unity and interdependence, while promoting an ethic of inter-being.

Transcension of subject-object duality: Refers to a shift away from the cognitive framing of dualism, including the individual as separate from the 'external' phenomenological world. The aim of transcension is also related to the immanence of being – i.e. to both acknowledge the role of individual personalities and their subjective influences while deepening into non-identified states of being.

Transition pathways: Indicates the desired shifts via paths-of-action from the meta-crisis to transformative possibilities.

Trans-rationality: A type of sense-making where rationality is incorporated but not elevated above other ways of knowing, sensing and being.

Temporal myopia: Refers to the human inability to comprehend the consequences of our actions through time.

BIBLIOGRAPHY

~

Abram, D. (2012). *The Spell of the Sensuous: Perception and language in a more-than-human world*. Vintage.

Agbo, N. (November 3, 2021). Restorative Economics: A Values-Based Roadmap to a Just Economy. *Nonprofit Quarterly*. Retrieved February 27, 2022, from: https://nonprofitquarterly.org/restorative-economics-a-values-based-roadmap-to-a-just-economy/

Akomolafe, B. (March 11, 2020). "Coming Down to Earth". *Bayo Akomolafe*. Retrieved March 30, 2021, from: https://www.bayoakomolafe.net/post/coming-down-to-earth

Akomolafe, B. (August 27, 2021). Interview with the authors

American Association of Geographers. (March 6, 2019). Rights of Nature: The New Paradigm. *American Association of Geographers*. Retrieved June 20, 2021, from: http://news.aag.org/2019/03/rights-of-nature-the-new-paradigm/

Anderson, B. (2006). *Imagined communities: Reflections on the origin and spread of nationalism*. Verso books.

Andreotti, V. (December 23, 2020). The Vital Compass: A conversation with Vanessa Andreotti, *The Dark Mountain Project*. Retrieved July 30, 2021, from: https://dark-mountain.net/the-vital-compass/

Anonymous. (February 7, 2021). Interview with the authors.

Anonymous. (June 14, 2021). Interview with the authors.

Anonymous. (July 22, 2021). Interview with the authors.

Anonymous. (September 21, 2021). Interview with the authors.

Anonymous. (October 3, 2021). Interview with the authors.

Arendt, H. (2013). *Hannah Arendt: The Last Interview: And Other Conversations.* Melville House

Asimov, I. (1983). *The foundation trilogy.* Ballantine Books.

Baldwin, J. (1962). Not everything that is faced can be changed, but nothing can be changed until it is faced. *American Essayist.* Retrieved May 5, 2022 from: http://www.quotehd.com/quotes/james-arthur-baldwin-quote-not-everything-that-is-facedcan-be-changed-but

Bansal, P. (November 9, 2021). Interview with the authors.

Barad, K. (2007). *Meeting the universe halfway: Quantum physics and the entanglement of matter and meaning.* Duke University Press.

Barad, K. (2010) 'Quantum entanglements and hauntological relations of inheritance: Dis/continuities, spacetime enfoldings, and justice-to-come', *Derrida Today,* 3(2): 240-268.

Barbara, A. *Time: Key concepts* (2004). Polity Press, UK. Harper Collins

Benyus, J. M. (1997). *Biomimicry: Innovation inspired by nature.*

Bernstein, N. O. (1986). *Beyond Objectivism and Relativism. Science, Hermeneutics, and Praxis.* University of Pennsylvania Press.

Bey, H (2003). *TAZ: The Temporary Autonomous Zone, ontological anarchy and poetic terrorism.* Autonomedia Press.

Bible, Holy. (1970). *The New American Bible.* New York, NY: Catholic Bible Publishers.

Bishop, M. & Green, M. (2010). *Philanthrocapitalism: How giving can save the world.* Bloomsbury Publishing USA.

Bohm, D (1980). *Wholeness and the Implicate Order.* Routledge.

Bollier, D & Helfrich, S. (2019). *Free, fair, and alive: The insurgent power of the commons.* New Society Publishers.

Bollier, D. (November 16, 2021). In Remembrance of My Dear Friend Silke Helfrich, 1967-2021. *David Bollier: News and perspectives on the commons.* Retrieved November 20, 2022, from http://www.bollier.org/blog/remembrance-my-dear-friend-silke-helfrich-1967-2021

Bookchin, M. (1982). *The Ecology of Freedom.* New Dimensions Foundation.

Bookchin, M. (1986). *Post-scarcity Anarchism.* The Anarchist Library. Retrieved May 22, 2022 from: https://theanarchistlibrary.org/library/murray-bookchin-post-scarcity-anarchism-book

Brand, D. (2002). *A Map to the Door of No Return: Notes to Belonging.* Vintage Canada.

Budge, W.E.A. and Wilson, E.A.M. (Eds.). (2016). *The Ancient Egyptian Book of the Dead.* Quarto Publishing, New York.

Buehler, J. (September 1, 2021). The complex truth about 'Junk DNA'. Quanta Magazine. Retrieved October 7, 2021, from:: https://www.quantamagazine.org/the-complex-truth-about-junk-dna-20210901/

Buen Vivir Fund. (September 29, 2021). Retrieved May 1, 2022, from https://thousandcurrents.org/buen-vivir-fund/

Buffett, J. (November 16, 2021). Interview with the authors.

Buffett, P. (26 July 2013). The Charitable-Industrial Complex. *New York Times*.

Buie, S. (12 July 2021). Interview with the authors.

Buis, A. (2019). A degree of concern: Why global temperatures matter. *NASA's Global Climate Change Website*, 19. Retrieved February 12, 2022, from: https://climate.nasa.gov/news/2865/a-degree-of-concern-why-global-temperatures-matter/

Butler, O. (2019). *The Parable of Talents.* Grand Central Publishing.

Camus, A. (2018). *The Myth of Sisyphus.* Knopf Doubleday Publishing.

Catton, W. (1982) *Overshoot: The ecological basis of revolutionary change.* University of Illinois Press.

Choksi, M. (2014), "Ancient Mesopotamian Beliefs in the Afterlife", *World History Encyclopedia*. Retrieved April 30, 2022, from: https://www.worldhistory.org/article/701/ancient-mesopotamian-beliefs-in-the-afterlife/

Climate Justice Alliance (2018). Just transition principles. *Climate Justice Alliance*. Retrieved February 10, 2021, from: https://climatejusticealliance.org/just-transition/

Cole, T. (2021, June 06). The white-savior industrial complex.*The Atlantic*. Retrieved April 30, 2022, from: https://www.theatlantic.com/international/archive/2012/03/the-white-savior-industrial-complex/254843/

Collaborative Authors. (April 24, 2010). People's Agreement of Cochabamba. *World People's Conference on Climate Change and the Rights of Mother Earth*. Retrieved February 13, 2021, from: https://pwccc.wordpress.com/2010/04/24/peoples-agreement/

Coppola, J. (June 30, 2010). Seals of Denial. *Truthout*. Retrieved February 15, 2021, from: https://truthout.org/articles/jason-coppola-seas-of-denial/

Culture Hack Labs. (December 2, 2020). Transforming the Transition Report. *Culture Hack Labs*. Retrieved December 2, 2020, from: https://www.culturehack.io/hacks/

Culture Hack Labs. (2021). *Narrative Report: the future is a territory we must defend (REV 1.1)*. Retrieved May 14, 2022, from https://curadaterra.org/wp-content/uploads/2021/10/Content-Labs-Indigenous-Futures-Report.pdf

Culture Hack Labs. (2022). About Page. *Culture Hack Labs*. Retrieved May 5, 2022, from: https://www.culturehack.io/about/

Daher, A. (December 12, 2021). The Valladolid debate, *Encyclopédie d'histoire numérique de l'Europe*, Retrieved April 30, 2022, from: https://ehne.fr/en/node/21394

Dayaneni, G. (November 19, 2021). Interview with authors.

de La Bellacasa, M. P. (2017). *Matters of care: Speculative ethics in more than human worlds* (Vol. 41). University of Minnesota Press.

Descartes, R. (2013). *Meditations on first philosophy*. Broadview Press.

Desjardins, J. (Ed.). (September 10, 2019). The $86 Trillion world economy – in one chart. *World Economic Forum*. Retrieved April 30, 2022 from: https://www.weforum.org/agenda/2019/09/fifteen-countries-represent-three-quarters-total-gdp/

Eisinger, J., Ernsthausen, J., & Kiel, P. (June 8, 2021). The Secret IRS Files: Trove of Never-Before-Seen Records Reveal How the Wealthiest Avoid Income Tax. *ProPublica*. Retrieved March 17, 2021 from: https://www.propublica.org/article/the-secret-irs-files-trove-of-never-before-seen-records-reveal-how-the-wealthiest-avoid-income-tax

Eliade, M. (1954). *Cosmos and History: The Myth of the Eternal Return.* Harper Torchbooks.

Ellis, N. (1988). *Awakening Osiris: A new translation of the Egyptian Book of the Dead.* Phanes Press, Boston MA.

Emerson, R. W. (2005, September 4). *Essays.* Retrieved May 4, 2022, from https://www.gutenberg.org/files/16643/16643-h/16643-h.htm#SELF-RELIANCE

Epstein, J. (February 17, 2022). Interview with authors.

Esteva, G. (August 26, 2021). Interview with authors.

Fleming, D. & Chamberlin, S.(Ed.). (August 4, 2016). *Surviving the Future: Culture, Carnival and Captial in the Aftermath of the Market Economy.* Chelsea Green Publishing.

Fisher, M (2009). *Capitalist Realism: Is there no alternative?.* Zero Books.

Forbes, J. D. (2011). *Columbus and other cannibals: The Wetiko disease of exploitation, imperialism, and terrorism.* Seven Stories Press.

Francis, M. (2020). Global Structures of Inequality and Unequal Distribution of Wealth. *Decent Work and Economic Growth, 490-498.* Cham: Springer International Publishing.

Gaia Amazonas. (June 8, 2020). What is the Indigenous Life Plan?. *Gaia Amazonas.* Retrieved March 5, 2021, from: https://www.gaiaamazonas.org/en/noticias/2020-08-06_what-is-the-indigenous-life-plan/

Galbraith, J. K. (2007). *The New Industrial State.* Princeton University Press.

Geertz, C. (1973). *The Interpretation of Cultures.* Basic Books

Giridharadas, A. (2019). *Winners take all: The elite charade of changing the world.* Vintage.

Global Justice Now. (2015). Corporations vs governments revenues: 2015 data. *Global Justice Now.* Retrieved April 10, 2021, from: https://www.globaljustice.org.uk/sites/default/files/files/resources/corporations_vs_governments_final.pdf

Global Justice Now. (2016). Ten biggest corporations make more money than most countries in the world combined. *Global Justice Now.* Retrieved March 7, 2021, from: https://www.globaljustice.org.uk/news/10-biggest-corporations-make-more-money-most-countries-world-combined/https://www.globaljustice.org.uk/news/10-biggest-corporations-make-more-money-most-countries-world-combined/

Ghosthorse, T. (June 12, 2021.). Interview with the authors.

Graeber, D. (2012). *Debt: The first five thousand years.* Melville House.

Graeber, D. (2018). *Bullshit Jobs: A theory.* Simon and Schuster.

Graeber, D. & Wengrow, D. (2021). *The dawn of everything: A new history of humanity.* Penguin UK.

Greene, B. (2003). *The Elegant Universe: Superstrings, hidden dimensions, and the quest for the ultimate theory.* W.W. Norton and Company.

Greer, C. (June 17, 2021). Interview with authors.

Hagens, N. Where Are We Going? *Resilience.* May 18, 2019. Retrieved April 30, 2022, from: https://www.resilience.org/stories/2018-05-08/where-are-we-going/

Haraway, D. (2016). *Staying with the Trouble: Making Kin in the Chthulecene.* Duke University Press.

Hartmans, A. (August 6, 2021). Mackenzie Scott's fortune has soared – even as she's become one of the world's leading philanthropists. *Business Insider.* Retrieved April 30, 2022, from https://www.businessinsider.com/mackenzie-scott-wealth-vs-dontions-chart-2021-8

Harvey, D. (2005) *A Brief History of Neoliberalism.* Oxford Press.

Hickel, J. (July 16, 2018.) Is it time for a post-growth economy?. *Al Jazeera.* Retrieved March 10, 2021, from: https://www.aljazeera.com/opinions/2018/7/16/is-it-time-for-a-post-growth-economy

Hickel, J. (2020). *Less is More: How degrowth will save the world.* Windmill Press, UK.

Hickel, J. (2021). The anti-colonial politics of degrowth, *Political Geography*, volume 88. Retrieved March 5, 2021, from: http://eprints.lse.ac.uk/110918/1/1_s2.0_S0962629821000640_main.pdf

Hooke, J & Mowll, J. (July 14, 2021). Interview with the authors.

Hyde, L. (2007). *The Gift: Creativity and the artist in the modern world.* Vintage Books.

Indie Philanthropy Initiative. (October 14, 2014). Methods. Retrieved May 2, 2022, from: https://indiephilanthropy.org/toolkit/methods/

Indigenous Action. (2020). *Rethinking the Apocalypse: An Indigenous Anti-Futurist Manifesto.* Retrieved March 11, 2021, from: https://indigenousaction.org/wp-content/uploads/rethinking-the-apocalypse-PRINT.pdf

Jamail, D. and Rushworth, S. (2022). We are in the middle of forever:*Indigenous Voices from Turtle Island on the Changing Earth.* The New Press.

James, T. (July 10, 2021). Interview with the authors.

Johnson, P.D. (2018). Global Philanthropy Report: Perspectives on the global foundation sector. *Harvard Kennedy School.* Retrieved April 14, 2021, from: https://cpl.hks.harvard.edu/files/cpl/files/global_philanthropy_report_final_april_2018.pdf

Justice Funders. (January, 2019). Just Transition for Philanthropy. Retrieved May 1, 2022, from: http://justicefunders.org/wp-content/uploads/2019/01/Spectrum_Final_12.6.pdf

Karpman, S.B. (2014). *A Game Free Life: The definitive book on the drama triangle and the compassion triangle by the originator and author.* Drama Triangle Productions

Kashtan, M. (November 25, 2016). You're Not a Bad Person: Facing Privilege Can Be Liberating. *Psychology Today*. Retrieved March 12, 2021, from: https://www.psychologytoday.com/us/blog/acquired-spontaneity/201611/you-re-not-bad-person-facing-privilege-can-be-liberating

Keller, C. (2014). *Cloud of the Impossible: Negative Theology and Planetary Entanglement (Insurrections: Critical Studies in Religion, Politics, and Culture).* Columbia University Press

Kothari, A. Salleh, A. Escobar, A. Demaria, F & Acosta, A. (Eds.). (2019). *Pluriverse: A post-development dictionary.* Columbia University Press.

Kimmerer, R.W (2015). *Braiding Sweetgrass: Indigenous wisdom, scientific knowledge and the teachings of plants.* Milkweed Editions.

Klein, N. (2015). *This Changes Everything: Capitalism versus the climate.* Simon and Schuster, UK.

Knight, B. (September, 28 2021). Interview with the authors.

Kramer, L. (January 4, 2021). Foundation Payout Policy in Economic Crises. *Stanford Social Innovation Review.* Retrieved July 15, 2021, from: https://ssir.org/articles/entry/foundation_payout_policy_in_economic_crises

Kramer, S.N. (1963). *The Sumerians: Their history, culture and character.* University of Chicago Press.

Krenak, A. (2020). *Ideas to Postpone the End of the World*. House of Anansi.

Ladha, A. (April 14, 2018). From "Green Growth" to Post-Growth. *Truthout*. Retrieved February 13, 2021, from: https://truthout.org/articles/from-green-growth-to-post-growth/

Ladha, A. (2019). Conscious Capitalism is an alibi and apology for our existing system. *Double Blind Magazine*. Retrieved February 13, 2021, from: https://doubleblindmag.com/conscious-capitalism-is-an-alibi-and-an-apology-for-our-existing-paradigm/

Ladha, A & Kirk, M. (March 19, 2015). Capitalism is Just a Story and Other Dangerous Thoughts, Part I. *Occupy.com*. Retrieved February 13, 2021, from: https://www.occupy.com/article/capitalism-just-story-and-other-dangerous-thoughts-part-i#sthash.2VDcx7M5.yFJdBFkD.dpbs

Ladha, A & Kirk, M. (March 19, 2015). Capitalism is Just a Story and Other Dangerous Thoughts, Part II. *Occupy.com*. Retrieved February 13, 2021, from: https://www.occupy.com/article/and-other-dangerous-thoughts-part-ii#sthash.NUiWp4V3.OtQMouKl.dpbs

Ladha, A., & Kirk, M. (2016). Seeing wetiko: On capitalism, mind viruses, and antidotes for a world in transition. *Kosmos Journal*. Retrieved February 13, 2021, from: Seeing Wetiko: On Capitalism, Mind Viruses, and Antidotes for a World in Transition – Kosmos Journal

Ladha, A, & Kirk, M. (February 24, 2020). The Poverty of Progress. *New Internationalist*. Retrieved February 13, 2021 from: https://newint.org/features/2020/02/24/poverty-progress

Ladha, A. (Autumn 2020). What is Solidarity? *Kosmos Journal*. Retrieved February 13, 2021, from: https://www.kosmosjournal.org/kj_article/what-is-solidarity/

Ladinsky, D. (Ed.) (2002). *Love poems from God: Twelve sacred voices from the East and West*. Penguin.

Latour, B (2018). *Down to Earth: Politics in the new climatic regime*. Polity Press, UK.

Lenel, L. (May 13, 2020). Public and Scientific Uncertainty in the Time of COVID-19. *History of Knowledge*, Retrieved June 1, 2021, from: https://historyofknowledge.net/2020/05/13/public-and-scientific-uncertainty/

Lessig, L. (2011). *Republic, Lost: How money corrupts Congress – and a plan to stop it*. Twelve Press.

Lipman, P. (21 January 2022). Interview with the authors.

Lovelock, J. E., & Margulis, L. (1974). Atmospheric homeostasis by and for the biosphere: the Gaia hypothesis. *Tellus, 26*(1-2), 2-10.

MacDougall, R. (2012). NIH Human Microbiome Project defines normal bacterial makeup of the body. *National Institute of Health*. Retrieved June 5, 2021, from: http://www.nih.gov/news/health/jun2012/nhgri-13.htmhttps://www.nih.gov/news-events/news-releases/nih-human-microbiome-project-defines-normal-bacterial-makeup-body#:~:text=The%20human%20body%20contains%20trillions,vital%20role%20in%20human%20health.

Machado de Oliveira, V. (2021). *Hospicing modernity: Facing humanity's wrongs and the implications for social activism*. North Atlantic Books.

Manji, F. (2019). *Emancipation, Freedom or Taxonomy? What does it mean to be African?. Racism After Apartheid: Challenges for Marxism and Anti-Racism*. Vishwas Satgar (Ed.). Wits University Press. Retrieved May 15, 2021 from: https://www.jstor.org/stable/10.18772/22019033061

Marya, R & Patel, R (2021). *Inflamed: Deep Medicine and the Anatomy of Injustice*. Farrar, Straus and Giroux.

McWhinney, W. (1997). *Paths of Change*. Sage Publications.

Meador, B.D.S. (1992). *Uncursing the Dark: Treasures from the underworld.* Chiron Publications, Wilmette, Illinois.

Menakem, R. (2017). *My Grandmother's Hands: Racialized trauma and the pathway to mending our hearts and bodies.* Central Recovery Press.

Miller, L. (June 29, 2012). The Money-Empathy Gap. *New York Magazine.* Retrieved March 17, 2021, from: https://nymag.com/news/features/money-brain-2012-7/

Monahan, M. (July 7, 2021). Interview with the authors.

Nagel, T. (1974). What is it like to be a bat. *Readings in philosophy of psychology, 1,* 159-168.

National Geographic. (September 22, 2020). The Five Major Types of Biomes. *National Geographic. Online Resource Library.* Retrieved March 21, 2021, from: https://www.nationalgeographic.org/article/five-major-types-biomes/

Nhất Hạnh, T. (1987). *Interbeing: Fourteen guidelines for engaged Buddhism.* Parallax Press

The NonProfit Times. (September 7, 2021). Foundation Spending Lags Investment Returns. *The NonProfit Times.* Retrieved September 24, 2021, from: https://www.thenonprofittimes.com/foundations/foundation-spending-lags-investment-returns/

Norberg-Hodge, H. (2000). *Ancient futures: learning from Ladakh.* Random House.

Öcalan, A. (2015). *Civilization, the Age of Masked Gods and Disguised Kings.* New Compass Press.

Patel, R. & Moore, J. (2018). *A History of the World in Seven Cheap Things: A Guide to Capitalism, Nature, and the Future of the Planet.* University of California Press.

Petroni, A. (January 15, 2021). Cooperation and chocolate: The story of one Colombian community's quest for peace. *Yes! Solutions Journalism.* Retrieved May 2, 2022, from: https://www.yesmagazine.org/economy/2021/01/14/harvesting-cacao-colombia-peace

Piketty, T (2014). *Capital in the 21st Century.* Harvard University Press.

Pinker, S. (2011). *The better angels of our nature: The decline of violence in history and its causes.* Penguin uk.

Pirsig, R.M. (1974). *Zen and the Art of Motorcycle Maintenance: An Inquiry into Values.* William Morrow and Company

Rasmussen, D.C. (June 9, 2016). The Problem With Inequality, According to Adam Smith. *The Atlantic.* Retrieved March 27, 2021, from: https://www.theatlantic.com/business/archive/2016/06/the-problem-with-inequality-according-to-adam-smith/486071/

Raygorodetsky, G. (November 16, 2018). Indigenous peoples defend Earth's biodiversity—but they're in danger. *National Geographic.* Retrieved April 3, 2021, from: https://www.nationalgeographic.com/environment/article/can-indigenous-land-stewardship-protect-biodiversity-

Rilke, R. M. & Mood, J.J.L. (Trans.) (1994). *Rilke on Love and Other Difficulties: Translations and Considerations.* W. W. Norton & Company.

Robinson, C. (May 9, 2021). The grantmaking practices we need. *Medium.* Retrieved May 1, 2022, from https://cassierobinson.medium.com/the-grantmaking-practices-we-need-142902ac0e5

Robinson, P. (2012). Top 1% Got 93% of Income Growth as Rich-Poor Gap Widened. *Bloomberg*. Retrieved February 5, 2021, from: https://www.bloomberg.com/news/articles/2012-10-02/top-1-got-93-of-income-growth-as-rich-poor-gap-widened

Rockström, J., Steffen, W., Noone, K., Persson, Å., Chapin III, F. S., Lambin, E., & Foley, J. (2009). Planetary boundaries: exploring the safe operating space for humanity. *Ecology and society*, *14*(2).

Rovelli, C (2014). *Reality Is Not What It Seems: The journey into quantum gravity*. Riverhead Books.

Sagan, D. (November 18, 2011). The human is more than human: Interspecies communities and the new "facts of life". *Cultural Anthropology*. Retrieved April 17, 2021, from: https://culanth.org/fieldsights/the-human-is-more-than-human-interspecies-communities-and-the-new-facts-of-life

Saul, J. R. (2013). *Voltaire's bastards: The dictatorship of reason in the West*. Simon and Schuster.

Schwab, T. (March 17, 2020). Bill Gates's charity paradox. *The Nation*. Retrieved September 18, 2021, from: https://cagj.org/2020/04/the-nation-bill-gatess-charity-paradox/

Seitz, K. & Martens, J. (2017). Philanthrolateralism: Private funding and corporate influence in the United Nations. *Global Policy*, *8*, 46-50. Retrieved May 22, 2022 from: https://docs.google.com/document/d/1pOOfDL1aHvAlJzBrPNoEteXEHrvafKleW1-RsP6BZWs/edit

Shafto, S.(2006). Leap into the Void: Godard and the Painter . *Senses of Cinema*. Retrieved 20 June 2022, from: http://www.sensesofcinema.com/2006/cinema-and-the-pictorial/godard_de_stael/#51

Sharpe, B. (2020). *Three horizons*. Triarchy Press.

Shaxson, N. (2011). *Treasure Islands: Tax Havens and the Men who Stole the World*. Vintage Press.

Shiva, V. & Shiva, K. (2020). *Oneness vs. the 1%: Shattering illusions, seeding freedom*. Chelsea Green Publishing.

Shiva, V. (Ed.). (2022). *Philanthrocapitalism and the Erosion of Democracy: A global citizens' report on the corporate control of technology, health, and agriculture*. Synergetic Press.

Shlain, L. (1998). *The Alphabet Versus the Goddess: The Conflict Between Word and Image*. Viking Press.

Snyder, G. (1974). *Turtle Island*. New Directions.

Smith, A. (2007). *The revolution will not be funded: Beyond the non-profit industrial complex*. INCITE.

Srivastava, G. P. (October-December 1967) The political and economic philosophy of Acharya Vinoba Bhave. *The Indian Journal of Political Science*, Vol. 28, No. 4, pp. 206-215.

Steverman, B., Melin, A. & Pendleton, D. (October 21, 2021) The Hidden Ways the Ultrarich Pass Wealth to Their Heirs Tax-Free. *Bloomberg BusinessWeek*. Retrieved October 30, 2021, from: https://www.bloomberg.com/features/how-billionaires-pass-wealth-to-heirs-tax-free-2021/

Stockholm Resilience Institute. Planetary boundaries. *Stockholm Resilience Institute Website*. Retrieved February 22, 2021, from: https://www.stockholmresilience.org/research/planetary-boundaries.html

Tamera Center. Outreach Partners Brazil. Favela da Paz in Brazil – transforming violence into music and community. *Tamera Peace Research and Education Center*. Retrieved May 2, 2022, from: https://www.tamera.org/favela-da-paz-brazil/

Tax Justice Network. FAQs. *Tax Justice Network Website.* Retrieved September 10, 2021, from: https://taxjustice.net/faq/how-much-money-is-in-tax-havens/

Taylor, A. (2019). Out of Time. *Lapham's Quarterly, Volume XII Issue 4* Retrieved 19 June 2021 from https://www.laphamsquarterly.org/climate/out-time .

Tennyson, A. T. B. (2013). The Complete Works of Alfred Lord Tennyson. Delphi Classics.

Thatcher, M. (September, 23 1987). Interview with Margaret Thatcher. *Woman's Own.* Retrieved July 3, 2021, from: https://www.margaretthatcher.org/document/106689

Theis, M. (November 9, 2021). Donor-Advised Funds Saw Rapid Growth in 2020. *Chronicles of Philanthropy.* Retrieved January 4, 2021, from: https://www.philanthropy.com/article/donor-advised-funds-saw-rapid-growth-in-2020?utm_source=Iterable&utm_medium=email&utm_campaign=campaign_3171463_nl_Philanthropy-Today_date_20211109&cid=pt&source=ams&sourceid=

Thiri, M. A., Villamayor-Tomás, S., Scheidel, A. & Demaria, F. (2022). How social movements contribute to staying within the global carbon budget: Evidence from a qualitative meta-analysis of case studies. *Ecological Economics, 195,* 107356. Retrieved March 30, 2022, from: https://www.sciencedirect.com/science/article/pii/S0921800922000180

Upaya Institute. (June 1, 2017). The Four great bodhisattva vows. *Upaya Institute and Zen Centter Website.* Retrieved May 8, 2022, from https://www.upaya.org/teachings/liturgy/four-great-bodhisattva-vows/

Vallely, P. (2020). *Philanthropy: From Aristotle to Zuckerberg.* Bloomsbury Publishing.
van der Wal, A. J., van Horen, F. & Grinstein, A. (2018). Temporal myopia in sustainable behavior under uncertainty. *International Journal of Research in Marketing, 35(3),* 378-393.

Varoufakis, Y. (June 28, 2021). Techno-Feudalism Is Taking Over. *Project Syndicate*. Retrieved July 7, 2021, from: https://www.project-syndicate.org/commentary/techno-feudalism-replacing-market-capitalism-by-yanis-varoufakis-2021-06

Villanueva, E. (2021). *Decolonizing wealth: Indigenous wisdom to heal divides and restore balance*. Berrett-Koehler Publishers.

Wahl, C.D. (July 7, 2017). The Three Horizons of Innovation and Culture Change. *Medium*. Retrieved April 30, 2022, from: https://medium.com/activate-the-future/the-three-horizons-of-innovation-and-culture-change-d9681b0e0b0f

Walker, D. (January 4, 2021) Unprecedented Times Call for Foundations to Take Unprecedented Actions. *Stanford Social Innovation Review*. Retrieved July 15, 2021, from: https://ssir.org/articles/entry/unprecedented_times_call_for_foundations_to_take_unprecedented_actions#

Wallerstein, E. (2014). *Historical Capitalism*, Verso.

Wang-Erlandsson, L., Tobian, A., Van der Ent, R., Fetzer, I., Te Wierik, S., Porkka, M., Staal, A., et al. (2022, April 26). A planetary boundary for Green Water. Retrieved April 30, 2022, from https://www.nature.com/articles/s43017-022-00287-8

Whitehead, A. (1967). *Modes of Thought*. The Free Press

Wolkstein, D. and Kramer, S.N. (1983). *Inanna: Queen of Heaven and Earth: Her stories and hymns from Sumer*. Harper & Row, New York.

Woodward, D. (2015). Incrementum ad Absurdum: Global growth, inequality and poverty eradication in a carbon-constrained world. *World Economic Review, 4, 43-62*.

World Bank. Current GDP (USD) Calculator.(2021) *World Bank Website*. Retrieved April 26, 2021, from: https://data.worldbank.org/indicator/NY.GDP.MKTP.CD?end=2020&start=1960

World Inequality Database (with a constant 2017 USD baseline). Retrieved April 26, 2021, from: https://wid.world

Xu, C., Kohler, T. A., Lenton, T. M., Svenning, J. C., & Scheffer, M. (2020). Future of the human climate niche. *Proceedings of the National Academy of Sciences, 117(21)*, 11350-11355. Retrieved June 4, 2021, from: https://www.pnas.org/content/117/21/11350

Yukteswar Giri, S.S. (2013). *The Holy Science.* Martino Fine Books.

Yusoff, K. (2018). *A Billion Black Anthropocenes or None.* University of Minnesota Press.

Zhongming, Z., Linong, L., Xiaona, Y., Wangqiang, Z., & Wei, L. (2019). Rights of Nature: The New Paradigm. *Global S&T Development Trend Analysis Platform of Resources and Environment.* Retrieved May 22, 2022 from: http://resp.llas.ac.cn/C666/handle/2XK7JSWQ/221100

94th Congress. (1975-1976). H.R.10612 – Tax Reform Act). *United States Congress.* Retrieved February 11, 2022, from: https://www.congress.gov/bill/94th-congress/house-bill/10612

∘ TRANSITION RESOURCE CIRCLE ∘

LYNN MURPHY

Lynn Murphy is a strategic advisor for foundations and NGOs working in the geopolitical South. She was a senior fellow and program officer at the *William and Flora Hewlett Foundation* where she focused on international education and global development. She resigned as a "conscientious objector" to neocolonial philanthropy. She holds an MA and PhD in international comparative education from *Stanford University*. She is also a certified *Laban/Bartenieff* movement analyst.

ALNOOR LADHA

Alnoor Ladha is an activist, journalist, political strategist and community organiser. From 2012 to 2019 he was the co-founder and executive director of the global activist collective *The Rules*. He is currently the Council Chair for *Culture Hack Labs*. He holds an MSc in Philosophy and Public Policy from the *London School of Economics*.

...

Lynn and Alnoor are co-directors of the *Transition Resource Circle*.

These are limited categories presenced to appease certain aspects of particular minds, including our own. We ourselves do not know who we fully are, and the omissions above belie the relational lines that co-constitute our "identities".

HEALING WEALTH IN THE TIME OF COLLAPSE

HEALING WEALTH IN THE TIME OF COLLAPSE

Printed and bound by CPI Group (UK) Ltd, Croydon, CR0 4YY
16/11/2023
03579733-0001